Offscreen

To advance humanity.

Welcome

As the people who create technology, we love to think of ourselves as the architects of a better tomorrow, an exciting future full of positive possibilities. We often believe that the fix for major problems is a technological one: where humans fail, let the machines figure it out. Technology is, by definition, progress. Or so we thought.

In the wake of global upheaval against the status quo, the tech community is coming to terms with having over-promised and under-delivered. Almost weekly, headlines about security breaches remind us that we're now in the post-privacy age, where private data is just another commodity. Meanwhile, a cultural shift is bringing deeply entrenched gender and racial inequalities into the open. And in Silicon Valley, unicorn defectors publicly apologise for having created addictive UI patterns and shady algorithms that exacerbate social division.

And just like that, the tech world finds itself on a soul-searching mission. The realisation that the ethical decisions made by its creators are baked into all technology has come as a surprise. It turns out that lifeless tools – such as a simple recommendation engine – are not as neutral or amoral as we thought. It's become clear now that programmers, designers, and data scientists are faced with some of the most pressing ethical dilemmas of our time. This forces us to ask a vital question: are they sufficiently equipped to make decisions on behalf of millions of people?

I would dare to say that we are on the cusp of a new era in technology. For the first time, we're seeing the broad ethical ramifications of the tools we build, sparking a discussion about what author Fabio Chiusi calls 'the human ghost in the machines'. From academics to journalists, and investors to politicians, we're finally starting to engage in the difficult conversations that could lead us to exciting and much-needed alternatives to the orthodoxies of the last few decades.

In a more enlightened era of tech, we will move beyond a superficial understanding of 'well designed', which today seems overly concerned with aesthetics. Instead, good design will focus on creating user experiences that are inclusive and empathetic, on writing code that is open and energy-efficient, and on running a business model that doesn't rely on infinite growth to survive.

Perhaps out of necessity, 'doing the right thing' for people, planet, and profit will soon have a much broader, mainstream appeal. Let's not forget that we – the industry at the forefront of change – carry a tremendous responsibility to lead the way. As the conversations and essays in this issue demonstrate, it is time that we all look inward and ask ourselves whether our work contributes to a tomorrow that will indeed be better than today.

Kai Brach
Publisher/Editor

Offscreen exists to remind us of technology's ultimate purpose: to advance humanity.

Publisher, Editor, Art Director
Kai Brach

Sub-Editor, Proofreader
Kieran O'Hare

Editorial Assistant
Ivana McConnell

Offscreen, Issue 18
First released in December 2017
ISSN 1839-891x

Published in Melbourne, Australia
Printed in Berlin, Germany
heftwerk.com

info@offscreenmag.com
www.offscreenmag.com
@offscreenmag

The main type family used is
Acumin Pro by Adobe. We print on
Circlematt White, a paper made from
100% recycled materials produced
with carbon-neutral energy and
certified by Germany's Blue Angel
and Europe's Flower eco-labels.

A fraction of Offscreen's cover
price is donated to The Australian
Conservation Foundation to support
environmental conservation projects.

Published three times per year, Offscreen is an independent print magazine with a thoughtful, human-centred take on technology and the web.

As a counterbalance to the endless stream of buzzword-heavy tech coverage, we dig deep into the backstories of creative ideas and successful companies. We celebrate innovation through introspective writing and authentic, human stories. We ask the big important questions about how we shape technology and how technology shapes us.

Our publishing efforts promote a tech and web community guided by ethical, sustainable, and inclusive principles. We are driven by strong values and a deep sense of purpose.

As a print-only title, we believe Offscreen is representative of where print is headed as a medium: instead of ad-driven publications for the masses, we'll see more niche titles in small print runs, created by zealous publishers with an appreciation for ink and paper. More than anything, this model depends on loyal readers that help spread the word and form a community around a publication they love.

Find out more about what we stand for:
offscreenmag.com/purpose

Support Offscreen by becoming a subscriber:
offscreenmag.com/subscribe

Contributors

Kamila Schneltser Pinilla
Kamila is a photographer based in Malmö, Sweden, whose work is a fusion between fashion and art. She believes in choosing a conscious way of living, and, inspired by great thinkers, she's on a quest to incorporate her ideals and values into her work.

Andy Forshaw
Andy is a graphic designer and illustrator who specialises in digital design, branding, and print. Based in the friendly city of Liverpool, he looks to create engaging, meaningful work for a wide variety of clients. When he's not crafting, he's most likely somewhere eating pizza.

Teresa Marenzi
Teresa is a Berlin-based photographer with a love for faces and natural light. Unless she's travelling for work, she's usually at home in Berlin-Kreuzberg, enjoying the local food and coffee scene or browsing art book stores.

Agnes Lee
Agnes is an illustrator in Brooklyn, New York. She is happiest when she is drawing. When she's not at her desk, she can be found camping in the mountains or chasing frisbees.

Derek Yarra
Derek is a portrait and fashion photographer with a passion for communicating human emotions through still images. Once a touring musician and always a competitive cyclist, he finds a way to balance all the things he loves while living in beautiful San Francisco.

Alice Default
Alice is a design producer and copywriter at Microsoft. Originally from France, she lived in Paris, Sydney, Palo Alto, and London before settling down in New York City. You can usually find her reading books, eating cheese, or confirming yet again that 'Default' really is her last name.

Sean McGeady
Sean is a sub-editor by day and asleep by night. If he's not culling copy for *Monocle*, he's probably working on his own independent publishing project, Castle, or pitching unjustified deep-dive analyses of stupid movies to exasperated editors. His interested include goats, snacks, and occult imagery.

Martin Holtkamp
Martin has been taking photos since he was given a monochrome polaroid camera by his godfather. He studied photography in Berlin and Bournemouth and moved to London in the early '90s. His work covers a range of genres, maintaining a minimalistic quality and style throughout. He now lives in Tokyo.

Shayan Asgharnia
Shayan is an editorial and advertising photographer currently living and working between Los Angeles and New York. From Questlove to Erin Brockovich, *The Wall Street Journal* to Macy's, Asgharnia is known for capturing the intrigue, magnetism, and depth in his subjects, creating a connection between them and the viewer.

18

Thoughts
Windows

It was my second morning in North Korea and it was not going well. The lights at the Yanggakdo International Hotel had been flickering, and eventually they went out altogether. I climbed the stairs to my room on the thirty-eighth floor, only to discover that I'd misplaced my ethernet adapter.

I needed to send critical correspondence to CNN before leaving for a symposium in just twenty minutes. Only five of us had SIM cards, so I couldn't group-text to ask for help. I didn't know how to describe the adapter to the North Korean hotel staff either. I would have to venture out and retrieve it myself. I glanced out the window as I left the room, high above the body of water that surrounded the hotel. Upon arrival, someone had murmured, *Alcatraz*.

I was in Pyongyang, the capital of the Democratic People's Republic of Korea, or DPRK. I was part of an international group of women on a peace mission to call for an end to the Korean War. Our journey would culminate in a walk across the Demilitarised Zone (DMZ). Among the thirty delegates were high-profile activists and Nobel Peace Laureates. A documentary film crew and journalists from The Associated Press and *The New York Times* made up the rest of our group of forty. I was there, somewhat bewilderingly, as communications director. The policy analyst and friend organising this women's march had asked me for help with design and social media strategy. I'd been a product designer at Twitter for many years, accustomed to building user experiences, but not to conducting press conferences from within one of the most isolated and mysterious places in the world.

Coleen is an artist and independent designer. She is an advisor at companies such as Medium and Sequoia Capital. Until late 2014, she was Staff Designer at Twitter, where she co-founded the Women In UX initiative (now Diversity in UX). In 2015, she worked as a field hand on an organic farm in Tuscany. She's lived in Seoul, Paris, and San Francisco, and she now resides in Manhattan, NY.

WORDS   ILLUSTRATION
Coleen Baik   Agnes Lee

In San Francisco, where smartphones and high connectivity abound, technology is both hyper-prevalent and invisible. It's the hum that runs under the surface of our lives, facilitating everything from getting somewhere to eating something to talking to someone. But I was rarely mindful enough of it to see it even as a convenience.

In Pyongyang I was constantly aware of technology: its cost, its limitations, the privilege required to get access to it. Only the elite had access to mobile devices, and data usage was restricted even for them. Around that time, all of North Korea combined had about the same internet traffic as a medium-sized office in the US. I had to pay $250 for a 3G connection, and $450 more for 2GB of data. Therefore, I was careful with my internet usage because I wanted to live-stream as much as I could from North Korea – if that was even going to be possible. I didn't have time to do things like check Twitter, anyway – I didn't have the time to be bored. I was also sharing this precious resource with others: one delegate borrowed my phone to connect with her husband, and a filmmaker checked her business emails while we were in transit. Technology was the fulcrum upon which so much seemed to balance.

When I was a kid, I loved watching the cartoon *Inspector Gadget*. The protagonist's niece, Penny, had a computer book and a video watch. I remember wanting that magic too, those forerunners to the iPad and the Apple Watch. Now they were commonplace, and I barely noticed that they existed.

Technology *is* magical. We forget, but the power and speed of our hand-held devices are astounding: today's cell phone has more computing capability than all of NASA had in 1969. It was once unimaginable to think of accessing GPS data, hiring a car, or having a face-to-face conversation through a sliver of metal we can hold in one hand.

In Pyongyang this magic was strikingly visible. A bit of glass and circuitry had reached its apotheosis, becoming much more than a phone – a lead rope in the night, a wormhole to another universe. It allowed seeing beyond physical and temporal boundaries. It had become a conduit of magic.

We pulled up to The Arch of Reunification, immense stone statues of women holding up a symbol for One Korea over the highway that leads from Pyongyang to the DMZ. I marveled, as I prepared to live-stream the beginning of this women's march, about how incredible it was to be the facilitator of this magic, the opener of this window between universes. I thought, also, about how this realisation was changing me. I wondered what other opportunities I miss daily because I'm unmindful of the immense potential of technology to connect and reveal.

We'd arrived. I was on edge and had tremors from lack of sleep as well as from nerves. I stepped off the bus and looked up. Hundreds of North Korean women stood in rows to send us off, their colourful dresses long and still in the thin light. I felt small. One of our delegates was already at the podium and had begun to speak: it was time. I opened up my magic window and lifted it high in the air, so that it could be flung open, far off on the other side of the world. ●

Thoughts
Inside Out

I look out past the bright lights and into the throng of diplomats and investors. Suits, ties, colourful pocket squares: it's a wash of well-meaning, middle-aged men, with a few authoritative women thrown into the mix. They grin back at me with parental encouragement, as if they were cheering on their kid at a high school talent show.

Except this isn't any normal auditorium. It's the United Nations. I'm here to moderate panels on blockchain – a term which only two years ago I might've thought was the name of an experimental Eastern European techno band. The people seated in front of me are some of the most influential brains in the field, and I'm about to lead them in a conversation that will be live-streamed to business leaders around the world. The opening question rattling around in my head is not part of my presenter notes: 'What the hell am I doing up here?'

Hi, my name's Georgia, and I'm a recovering lifestyle journalist. During my eight years working in high-end culture and design magazines, there was always a VIP pass waiting for me backstage, my closet overflowed with free shoes, and my champagne glass was always full. I skipped lines, befriended celebrities, and never had to make dinner reservations.

I loved my time working in that realm, but not because of the freebies. Those years taught me about people: what they liked, what they feared, and who they covertly wanted to be. The pages I curated allowed readers to imagine a different, idealised version of themselves, one free of the banalities of everyday life.

But my personal form of escapism was different. While my days were filled with Scandinavian lighting designers and nouveau

Georgia is an editor who focuses her human-centric lens on emerging technologies. A former lifestyle journalist who spent three years as the editor of *Kinfolk* magazine and edited a *New York Times* best-selling design book, she recently surrendered to her inner nerd and is now an Ideas Editor at Quartz in New York.

Brutalist architecture, my evenings were spent studying quantum computing and reading up on the latest developments in gene editing. Outside of business hours, Elon replaced *Elle*, Kurzweil replaced Kenzo, deGrasse Tyson replaced de Kooning. I was turning to tech.

At first, I felt like I couldn't tell anyone – liberal arts types don't usually hang out with data scientists. Since I lacked the language of Python or CSS, I had to communicate through the only other means I knew: people. My time as an editor had taught me to take a step back, assess the zeitgeist, and ponder how trends influence society. I found myself doing the same with emerging technologies. Would this new thing make us more productive or more anxious, more connected or more disengaged?

I was surprised by how little introspective, human-centred discussion there was about the future of technology. The deeper I dove, the more obvious the implicit biases became: machine-learning algorithms trained on datasets of wealthy, white men; voice-controlled interfaces spitting out tone-deaf, gendered tropes; a giant income gap that left women earning up to a third less than their male counterparts.

If technology was a vision of the future, it was a myopic one. And a lack of alternative perspectives was part of the problem. Hiding my newfound nerdy passion only further entrenched the belief that young, cortado-sipping design types didn't have an interest in becoming programmers and engineers. Not wanting to further that stereotype for yet another generation, I decided to quit my job, relinquish my fancy lifestyle, move back to New York, and give in to my geeky self – with pride.

At first, I was worried that no one would take me seriously, but I quickly realised that my outsider status played to my advantage. Years of editing gave me the ability to take dense blocks of information and convert them into accessible, relatable stories. I became an interpreter between the technologists and the people who use the technology.

If my career change taught me one thing, it's that the tech world needs more outsiders. We need more people who are brave enough to admit their ignorance and are willing to try applying their skill set to a new set of problems. Imagine what VR game designers could learn from theatre set builders who intimately understand immersive experiences. Imagine what social media managers could learn from social workers who appreciate the fragility of healthy communities. Imagine what AI developers could learn from contemporary philosophers who can offer historical insights into human desire and morality.

On stage that day at the UN, I didn't pretend to be an expert. Instead, I chose to be curious. I asked questions I didn't know the answers to. I probed about blockchain's real-world impact. I pressed them to explain *why* we should care about it. Sitting up there amidst some of the world's smartest techies, I remembered why I got into this industry in the first place: to make people feel included and optimistic about the future, not ostracised and hopeless. But if emerging technologies are truly to change the world, it must be a conversation, not a keynote.

Now taking questions from the audience… ●

WORDS
Alice Default
Ivana McConnell
Kai Brach

Projects
Ideas Worth Exploring

1
Data-driven promise tracking
Promise Tracker puts the data (and the power) into citizens' hands, keeping governments accountable for promises they make. Within the app, a community group can design a mobile survey to identify local issues, then easily visualise and take action on the results – including monitoring how well government responds.
promisetracker.org

2 →
The floating rubbish bin
Seabin's inventor calls it a rubbish bin for the ocean. It's a humble concept, but with huge implications: the Seabin V5 unit is a floating debris collection device, powered by a small submersible water pump. It pulls in and catches 1.5kg of floating debris each day in a biodegradable catch bag. A drop in the ocean? Perhaps, but that's half a ton of rubbish per year that's not floating in the world's waters.
seabinproject.com

3 →

Culture hopping

Imagine experiencing different cultures by just stepping into a shipping container. From Kabul to Baltimore, Nairobi to Mexico City, Shared Studios paints shipping containers gold and equips them with immersive audio-visual technology before opening these 'Portals' to local communities. Once you step inside, you come face-to-face with a person in another Portal somewhere else in the world. Designed to learn, teach, share, play, and connect, Portals aim to make the world a smaller place. sharedstudios.com

4

Next-gen pocket money

It's never too early to learn how to properly manage your money. At least, that's the thinking behind Pennybox, an app that lets kids earn and save money by doing jobs and tasks around the home. Tasks are submitted by both parents and kids, attached to a dollar value. Once completed, kids can collect and track their money before finally cashing out. Set your kids up for a healthy financial future – all while getting them to do the dishes. pennybox.com

5 ←

Smarter energy consumption

Through a sensor that connects to pretty much any electricity meter, Wattcost tracks your energy consumption in real time and sends you notifications when costly appliances are left on or the fridge door is left open. It also helps you find the most affordable energy plan that's best suited to your needs. Launched through a crowdfunding campaign, Wattcost currently ships to Australia and New Zealand only. wattcost.com

6 →

High-tech beekeeping
BuzzBox is trying to harness the power of tech to fight the alarming decline of the world's bee population. This solar-powered beehive sensor tracks the health of a hive by analysing temperature, humidity, and even audio recordings of the buzzing of bees. By detecting diseases, parasites, a missing queen, or other health issues, beekeepers can act more quickly to save their hives.
osbeehives.com

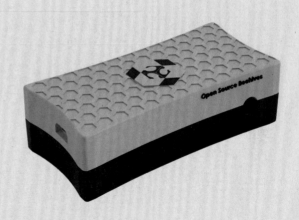

7 ↓

Trees by drones
BioCarbon Engineering builds tree-planting drones to help fight deforestation. Their drones can carry 300 biodegradable seed pods at once and cover one hectare in just eighteen minutes in any type of landscape, planting a tree every six seconds. Realising that 500 billion trees could offset all human carbon emissions, they've committed to planting an impressive one billion trees per year.
biocarbonengineering.com

8

A better way to browse
Brave is a new browser on a mission to fix the internet. At its helm is Brendan Eich, inventor of Javascript and co-founder of Mozilla. As an open-source browser, Brave promises less clutter (no cookies, ads, or trackers), safer browsing, and faster loading times on laptop and mobile. It also lets you donate to your favourite websites in bitcoin with a monthly browsing budget that you set yourself.
brave.com

9 ←

Mobile eye scans
Peek Retina makes eye exams
possible anywhere in the world.
A small camera attaches to any
smartphone and transforms
it into a portable ophthalmo-
scope to examine the optic nerve
and detect eye diseases. Easy
enough to use by non-health-
care professionals for screening
vision problems, Peek Retina
makes professional-grade
eye check-ups accessible to
people in remote rural areas.
peekvision.org

10

Wikipedia, simplified
Wikipedia is a wonderful treasure trove of knowledge, but its
academic format can make it difficult for adults with a learning
or reading disability, or for people with English as their
second language. Simple English Wikipedia offers an alternative version with shorter sentences and simplified words and
grammar. It takes complex ideas and articles from the regular
English Wikipedia and makes them accessible to anyone.
simple.wikipedia.org

11 →

Crows as a cleaning crew
Could crows be trained to rid our cities of cigarette butts? The people behind Crowded Cities
believe so. With Crowbar they've designed an
intelligent trash bin that dispenses bird food
in exchange for cigarette filters. Butts dropped
at the bottom of the bin are recognised by
the built-in camera. Currently on trial in the
Netherlands, the Crowbar is a natural and cheap
step towards cleaning up one of the most trou-
blesome contributors to litter on this planet.
crowdedcities.com

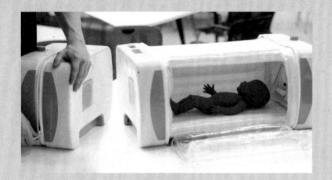

13
Offline messaging
Based on peer-to-peer mesh networking technology, FireChat is an app that lets you message
the people around you without requiring any
signal, data plan, or internet connection. By using
the radios inside our phones to connect them
directly with one another, encrypted messages
are passed from one phone to another (if they're
less than 210 feet apart) until they reach their
recipient. A free and community-based alternative that has found a particularly passionate
following in areas with low network coverage.
opengarden.com

12 ←
Portable incubators
When design student James
Roberts came across a short
documentary on the alarmingly
high death rate for prema-
ture babies born in Syria,
he used his final university
project to come up with a
solution: mOm incubators can
be easily inflated to provide
infants with a protective,
heated environment that is
backed up by battery power.
momincubators.com

14 →
The smokeless fire pit
Camping gets an upgrade with
this new fire pit. Designed to
minimize smoke through a blue-
tooth-controlled air injection
system, this portable wood-
and charcoal-burning pit also
cooks your meals, recharges
your phone, and is beautiful to
look at. Sales of the FirePit also
support one of the company's
other projects: the HomeStove,
a safer wood-burning cookstove
made for households across
India and sub-Saharan Africa.
bioliteenergy.com

15

Critical health alerts when it counts

In the case of an emergency, shortly after you arrive at a hospital, mobile app Iris goes into alert mode, displays your personal health information, and notifies your pre-defined emergency contacts via text message. Iris makes sure doctors know about your allergies, donor status, and any other important health issues in case you're unconscious.
getiris.co

16 →

Light made from gravity

As a sustainable alternative to kerosene lamps, Gravity Light replaces polluting, dangerous, and expensive lighting for people in the developing world. Powered by nothing but gravity, the lamp works through the connection of a weight to a pulley system that slowly powers a generator as the weight falls to the ground. Currently distributed in Kenya, the charity behind it is working with local sales agents and community networks to scale its distribution.
gravitylight.org

17 ←

Machine learning for crops

What if a simple photo could save crops from succumbing to pests and diseases? Through machine learning and image recognition, paired with a global online community, Plantix helps small farmers to identify unwanted fungi and insects, and then find solutions to the problems they cause by simply uploading a picture of their affected crops. Created for farmers who can't afford human consultants, the app and database are already being accessed more than a million times per month.
plantix.net

18 ↑
Clean teeth, clean planet
Be has all the benefits of an electric toothbrush without requiring an electrical outlet for charging. It's powered by you – not batteries. With just two twists of the dial at the bottom of the toothbrush, Be gives you a full two-minute professional-level teeth cleaning.
thegoodwellcompany.com

19
Web citizenship
Citizen Ex is a browser extension that shows you where the websites you visit reside and how that affects your legal rights. Based on your browsing patterns, the plug-in breaks down your identity into a series of country percentages, compiling your 'algorithmic citizenship'. It offers a glimpse into how your internet usage is viewed by web services, companies, and governments.
citizen-ex.com

20 ←
Life-giving box
OffGridBox is an all-in-one system that provides sustainable energy and safe water, all while fitting inside a small shipping container. It helps NGOs, schools, businesses, and homeowners alike, and is able to support anything from cabin living to an entire rural village in developing countries. The unit only takes a few hours to install and requires minimum training to operate and maintain.
offgridbox.com

21 →
A safer, smarter phone
Blackphone is a smartphone built for the privacy-minded. Claiming to be one of the most secure smartphones on the planet, Blackphone provides features like anonymous search, privacy-enabled bundled apps, more control over in-app permissions, and of course private, encrypted communication. Still want to play Angry Birds or check your Gmail account? Blackphone provides spaces for you to separate your work and personal lives without sharing sensitive data between the two.
silentcircle.com

22
Visualising the world through AI
With its research project Seeing AI, Microsoft is taking text-to-speech intelligence for the blind and visually impaired one step further. On top of reading all text and documents that you put in front of your phone's camera, this mobile app also puts words on the world around you. Just point your phone and it will recognise products by their barcodes, or a smile on a human face, or a waiting taxi in the street. Microsoft calls it a glimpse of the future, and it might be just that.
microsoft.com

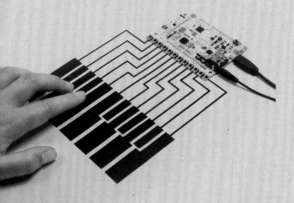

23 ←
Powerful paint
With Bare Conductive, any object or surface – including your skin – can become an interactive sensor. This water-based and skin-safe conductive paint, with the wide array of different kits on offer, can turn a wall into a light-switch, hands into piano keys, or your stairs into a security alarm against intruders. ●
bareconductive.com

Craig Mod

The writer and his quest for
quiet space in a noisy world.

INTERVIEW
Kai Brach

PHOTOGRAPHY
Martin Holtkamp

Craig is a digital savant in love with the analogue. In code, design, and photography, but mostly through his writing, he explores our collective struggle to find focus in a world of perpetual distraction. Rather than seeking commercial success, he prefers living a quiet life in a seaside town south of Tokyo – sometimes escaping to remote writing retreats around the US – where he revels in his various creative outlets while hidden from the public eye. When he's ready, he emerges from hibernation with thought-provoking, introspective essays, books, and talks that examine the meaning of a connected life.

Let's get a couple of key questions out of the way first: how would you describe the current state of the book as a medium? If print is not dead, and ebooks are not what they promised to be, where are we headed from here?

Well, what's clear is that Amazon won, and that did a few things. First, it ossified the state of ebooks, with Amazon having a de-facto monopoly on that medium. When you are competing against Kindle, it's very difficult to grab a significant enough amount of the market to make it rational for a venture capitalist to give you money. As a result of that, ebooks are stagnant right now.

Seven years ago, this space felt invigorating. Remember Nook, Kobo, or iBooks on the newly launched iPad? Lots of people got really excited about what a digital reading experience could look like. Flipboard emerged out of that era too. But now that the Kindle plays the most prominent role, all these other ideas have died out or gotten swallowed up by Amazon. And the Kindle turns out to be a good enough solution for enough people, which means it's not evolving at all. So here we are.

I did a calculation earlier this year: Kindle sales and book sales in general now account for less than *one per cent* of Amazon's market cap. The Kindle could disappear tomorrow, and Amazon would not, in any way, be affected. As a company with the best interests of shareholders in mind, it's clear that putting money into innovating ebooks is not a worthy investment for them. What drives a lot of traditional publishing houses, though, is not necessarily financial returns. It's respect for the medium and recognising its cultural importance. I mean, you're probably not making a ton of money publishing an indie magazine, right? Sadly, I don't get the impression that the publishing arms of Amazon or Apple operate under that ethos.

What's good about all this is that the publishing industry is now able to relax a bit. Seven years ago, there were a lot of question marks. Is print going to survive? Which platform should we build for? Oh my god, do we need an apps division? Now, it's OK. There's Kindle. That's it. We can kind of ignore everything else. Nobody wants apps. And guess what? Print sales are going up again and indie bookstores are seeing a resurgence. Turns out things aren't that different than they were ten years ago, just that we now have Amazon as the uber-ubiquitous distribution vector for print and digital.

What do you think drives a reader's decision to go for either the printed or the digital edition?

I'm not sure if readers spend a lot of time consciously thinking about that choice. Personally, I think Kindle Samples are a game changer. I don't buy books unless I read the samples now. That's my threshold. If I can't get through the sample, I won't buy the book. If I *really* like it, then I usually buy the physical book.

I think the return of print is in line with all the other movements towards offline activities – things like vinyl records, Moleskins, expensive pens, et cetera. Anything that gets you away from the screen has gone up in value.

But I think books are the ultimate entertainment experience when it comes to having quiet, non-screen time. There is no other medium that gives you hours of quiet enjoyment. Even with vinyl LPs, where one side lasts for around twenty minutes, you are constantly made aware of the medium; whereas a book offers this fully immersive, quiet experience for hours or days. It's certainly more quiet than a newspaper, which makes you aware of all the horrors in the world all the time.

When it comes to making time for reading and writing, do you have a set of self-imposed rules you try to adhere to?

My entire life is basically structured around trying to make space for thinking. Everything I do, all the decisions in my life, kind of boil down to that. Because I'm really wimpy. Just like so many of us, I'm weak when it comes to resisting the bounty of online goodness.

When you sit down with a book, you understand the parameters of that engagement. You know how long the book is. The book isn't changing as you read it. It's a solid, immutable thing. You and the book are on equal terms in some ways. You know what's going to happen, and the book abides by its contract, which is being a book.

In the digital realm, however, some games and apps quickly turn into slithering creatures

under your feet. You never know where you stand. Everything is constantly being optimised to pull you back in for one more minute, one more click. All those chemical reactions in your brain that tell you to keep going – I feel that very strongly when I am online.

That's why I try to create ways to subvert my weaknesses – by turning off the internet, for instance. When I go to bed at night, the internet goes off. It doesn't come back on until after lunch the next day, at least. The difference in the quality of the day ahead between starting my morning with the internet on versus off is enormous. If I wake up and the first thing I do is look at my phone, I've lost hours, and not even because I'm sitting there browsing social media: it's hours of thinking time. The addict part of my brain takes over and prevents me from being quiet and thoughtful and contemplative. I just lose that ability to dive into other worlds, the worlds of writing or programming or design.

How has the omnipresence of the internet changed the rules of becoming a writer?

The barriers are much lower, of course. It's way more democratic. Today, if you put in the legwork, you can be a writer. A similar shift has happened in photography, where thirty years ago you had to spend tens of thousands of dollars on equipment. Today, you can make a name for yourself as a photographer with just your mobile phone.

The power of the internet has always been to connect people within certain subcultures, people who don't have as strong a voice in mainstream media. Writers have taken advantage of that from the early days of the internet, voicing unique opinions and finding their audience through that medium.

The flip side of that process of democratisation is that making money with writing is really hard, because so many people are willing to do it for next to nothing. Most writers today are also incentivised to write things that primarily get clicks, which can be a good forcing function but doesn't always lead to great quality.

I've been reading about John McPhee's process of writing these giant essays for

The New Yorker thirty or forty years ago, and wow, it feels like an alien world. His process is so slow and deliberate. At the end, he would hand in an eighty-thousand-word piece. That's a book! Whatever structure allowed McPhee to write that way back then, it barely exists today. There's hardly ever enough white space, enough thinking time today, to process information the way he was able to.

You largely focus on writing today, but your interests cover lots of different creative fields, including design, photography, and programming. Which one of those came first?

Writing and design have always been weirdly present throughout my life and so has technology. I started programming when I was eight or nine years old, mainly because I wanted to make games. Even more than programming I liked the idea of designing games and game characters. At the same time, I was obsessed with Stephen King's *The Dark Tower* series which I read when I was in fourth or fifth grade. There was something about that narrative that I couldn't get out of my head.

My teenage years were a mix of that: designing, programming, writing short stories, and eventually discovering the internet where I was running BBSs and playing around with building websites. I was also co-running a small publishing company in the early 2000s. For me that was a way to get really close to books without actually having to write them. It taught me a lot about design and mastering the limits of that space. Moving to Japan only fortified my curiosity about books. Japan does physical books so well, does paper so well! It had a massive influence on me.

Was there a turning point when you realised that writing was your thing?

There was, actually. In 2009 I hiked up to Annapurna base camp in Nepal where I met a lot of wonderful people. I had an incredible bonding experience with my guide who became like a brother to me. As I came down to Kathmandu, I was really overwhelmed with emotions. At the time I was also struggling to process a lot of different events in my life and so I drank myself into such a blackout that I woke up the next morning with a big gash on my head and a distinct feeling of fluid behind my ear.

I flew back to Tokyo and straight to the emergency room to get an MRI. Thankfully everything was all right, but I knew some demons needed to be addressed. This weird, tumultuous internal strife or angst – whatever it was – was holding me back from realising what I wanted to realise in life. I felt very constrained. I felt like I didn't have any archetypes or any mentors that I could look towards. As an attempt to process some of these thoughts, I decided to fully give

Current location
Kamakura, Japan

Hometown
Hartford, CT, USA

Top bookmarks
washingtonpost.com,
news.ycombinator.com,
techmeme.com

Top apps
Google Maps, Camera,
Safari, Hacker News,
Snapseed

Recommended reading
Train Dreams by Denis
Johnson, *Stone Animals*
by Kelly Link, *An Artist
of the Floating World*
by Kazuo Ishiguro

Inspired by
Kevin Kelly: my touchstone
archetype of a relentlessly
curious person who melds
literature, business, family,
and photography – all
tempered by the kindest
of patient hearts.

Favourite accessory
Koyasan Jizu wrist beads:
the entirety of the Heart
Sutra is carved onto
them, and they remind me
no matter how bonkers
stressed you may be, two
nights in a good mountain
temple can help realign
your dumb monkey brain.

Tea or coffee
Coffee, hot and black

On the web
craigmod.com

myself up to writing about the complicated
experience I had just had on that mountain.

During my hike I had captured many amazing
moments with a new Panasonic GF1 camera.
This camera and the photos I shot became a
big online essay. It took me months to write
and design that piece, but when I finally
published it on my site, I remember crying
looking at the response. It was incredible.

The essay was a camera review – a camera
field test – but written in a kind of personal
way that was unheard of at the time. Through
affiliate links in that single post I sold enough
of those cameras to pay for two or three years
of living. But more importantly, psychologically,
for me it was a major turning point. I realised that words can have a powerful impact,
connecting me with a much bigger audience
than anything else I had ever done before.

Two months after that, I published another
essay called *Books in the Age of the iPad* just
before I got on a plane to New York. By the time
I landed, it had been picked up by *The New York
Times* and I had two book offers in my inbox.

Wow, what a flying start to a new career!

It sounds like an overnight success story, but it took seven years of making books to be able to think about writing that post about books – and even then, six months of *actual* writing and editing and rewriting to complete it. The response I got turned out to be an important external validator.

This idea that you just have to be internally driven to get somewhere good, it's bullshit. Locking yourself into a room for weeks or months to get your thoughts out is tough. It's lonely. It's dark. And sometimes you want to drink yourself into the ground. That's why getting external validation can be really powerful – not as the sole purpose of working hard but as a nudge that says, 'You're on the right track!' When you're going through a rough patch and start doubting yourself, you can look back at those achievements reassuringly: 'At one point, I really knew what I was doing, so let's keep going. Let's have faith in this thing I'm working on now and hope this one works out too.'

Some time after writing those essays you took on a design role at Flipboard, but you eventually went back to being independent so that you could focus on writing. Was working for a tech company not what you expected?

Working with Marcos Weskamp at Flipboard was great and I learned a lot, but it became clear to me that the biggest return on the time I put into the world was codifying and solidifying my ideas and experiences into the form of essays and books.

Most of what I do is structured around return on investment. And I don't mean that coldly. I mean that in the sense of respect for life itself. We are alive. We have consciousness. We are capable of creative and intellectual output like no other creature on this planet. I think we tend to forget how amazing and weird and magical that is.

So I ask myself regularly, 'Am I maximising my respect for being alive or not?' And the best way I've found for me to say 'yes' to this question is by putting what's in my head into words. I know this all sounds hippie-dippy, but it's a really good organising function for thinking about what we should be doing in life.

And even the absurd amounts of money offered to a talented person like yourself didn't make you think twice?

There was just no company in Silicon Valley where the return on investment from being there was going to be as great as the return from the things I wanted to do. Living in San Francisco would have made me feel like an insane person. There is just no support or understanding for the stuff I want to work on. Everyone constantly asks how I could refuse a well-paid creative director's job at an ad platform.

So I moved back to Japan, a place where I'm interacting with people who are doing work that may not pay a lot, but that adds a significant cultural positive to their town, city, or country. Here, the cost of living isn't very high. I don't need a giant paycheck every month to cover my basic expenses. I don't spend ten thousand dollars a month to rent a tiny apartment. I don't need a hundred-thousand-dollar car.

This is not about being austere for austerity's sake, but it goes back to the question, 'How do I make sure I'm giving time and focus to the things that I feel are respecting life?' Making sure my fixed cost of living is as low as possible removes the problem of having to do certain jobs just to pay for a particular lifestyle. Living in a country with good healthcare also means that you don't have to worry about how you can afford treatment if some kind of health tragedy strikes. That's a great bonus.

You regularly disappear to 'writing retreats' and you spend weeks or months in a remote location working on a book or an essay without much contact with the outside world. It sounds like a pretty radical way of removing distraction.

Just to explain what these retreats are: they are basically writing fellowships provided by endowments to private, non-profit institutions. You submit complicated, onerous applications and gather letters of recommendation and then hope that a panel of judges selects you. If you get in, everything is paid for. They give you lodging and a studio to work in. It's mainly for writers, but there are also photographers, painters, composers, et cetera.

There's very little internet access. It's about living with a piece of text or a story and getting the time and space to do deep work in a way that you could never do in everyday life. These retreats are wonderful,

because you are surrounded by equally insane people doing equally insane things. You don't ask, "What are you working on?" You ask, "How many years are you on?" And then you realise that there are people that have been working on a book for five or ten years.

It's about being around people who are doing wildly creative things in wildly non-commercial contexts on stupid timelines. You take a lot of energy from that. These retreats give you a support network. They make you feel less crazy and they remind you that there is value to the work you are doing, that success *can* be measured in different ways.

In America, our baseline for measuring success is money. Money has become a horrible proxy for intelligence. Your human value is whatever is in your bank account. One of the great joys of living in Japan is that here, your value is not about money, but about dedication and commitment to the institution. That institution could be a big company, like Hitachi or Mitsubishi, but it could also be the art of knife-making or paper-making. In

that sense, the way individuals are valued in Japan feels very similar to how people treat each other during those retreats in America.

In one of your essays you describe going offline for such a long period as a privilege. Does that mean that in the future going offline will be a luxury that only rich people like you or me can afford?

I think it already is. What average office worker can ignore their emails for a week? The irony is that for people like Jack Dorsey, the CEO of Twitter, it's probably easier to go offline for a week than it is for a designer working at Twitter.

Our default expectation is now 'always available.' The systems we created are now so frictionless that we haven't noticed how insidious they have become in keeping us hooked. It's like the 'boiling frog' parable: step by step, we're optimising ourselves to maximum productivity without realising how much it actually hurts us. At the same time it's all become very abstract. As an employer with a global workforce,

you have no idea where your employees might be right now or what they might be doing, so you just expect them to answer immediately. The concept of downtime is elusive.

So, yeah, it's already a great privilege to be able to say 'no' to that.

Do you see a possible future where this trend is reversed?

Personally, I don't. If you peel back the layers, you see how it returns to the structure of capitalism. It's all about short-term time scales focused on numbers: growth of users, growth of engagement, growth of revenue. There is no morality baked into that structure, so there are no incentives for companies trying to reverse this trend.

Instead of searching for some unicorn of balance, I have found one easy solution: unplugging my router. All of a sudden I can think again, I can focus. I know that may sound hyperbolic to some, but it's one of those things that you don't recognise how powerful it is until you have done

it a few times. It's all about bridging the intellectual and experiential gap. Intellectually, you know you'll be able to get more and better work done by going offline. To experience the benefits, you just have to be disciplined enough to do it something like fifty times. Then, eventually, you come to recognise the nuances in the way you think about things, your insights into problems, and the quality of the solutions you come up with. Whether it's writing, programming, or design, it's a completely different space of thinking.

You seem like a person who's very easily excited about new technologies, but you're also deeply curious about traditional craftsmanship and an obsessively detailed, slow creative process. Are those contradictory interests?

Well, tech doesn't inherently have to be super fast. You don't *have to* 'move fast and break things.' That's not an immutable law of technology; that's a law of Silicon Valley. It's important not to conflate the two. Though I think that, in terms of creating a culture of exploring intellectual ideas as connected to technology, Silicon Valley is incredible.

There are obvious issues with venture capitalism and how it can breed these complex platforms that become weaponised over time, like we've seen in recent years. But it's silly to just point at $150-million smart juicers and paint an entire field with the same brush.

I'm not at all interested in any of the flashy stuff – like a new dating app or a smart door lock. Those are companies that are operating in the context of pure venture capitalism. For me, the most exciting, interesting technology is quiet. It's in the background. And it's not necessarily consumer-facing.

I'm thinking of Bret Victor's lab in Oakland, where he has been exploring – very deliberately and quietly – new modes of physical computing. And he's doing so by using really boring technologies: a constellation of networked cameras and projectors deployed in interesting, smart ways. That's incredibly fascinating. So I think the same philosophies of quietude and disconnection and silence can be applied to technology. In fact, they should be.

That said, I believe the philosophies around quick iteration can be important outside of the shark tank of fast consumer tech. Iterating quickly can be an effective way of working through ideas. One of the greatest dangers to any creative project is allowing the potential for the thing to subvert your ability to make it, because you want to live in a world of potentiality for as long as possible. A book is always greatest before it's written. You are intoxicated by what it can be. That's very dangerous. You want to kill those seductions as quickly as possible, and one way to achieve that is fast iteration.

So the release of the latest iPhone model doesn't get you excited?

I'm generally more dismayed about consumer tech than excited. The iPhone? The camera keeps getting better, that's about it. The tool, as it stands, kind of hit its apex in its third or fourth generation. Today, we get slightly faster ways to use Instagram or Twitter.

Rather than any new feature, what's way more interesting is the trickle-down effect of those consumer technologies. How does the commodification of components within the iPhone affect research? What does it enable in developing countries where those third or fourth generations are now affordable?

Going back to your writing, one concept that pops up regularly is the idea of things – whether real or intangible – having clear 'edges'. Can you explain what you mean by that?

You can even describe my obsession with going offline as an attempt to give my life edges, if you will. Having a bounded mental space that I have full control over.

In my writing and talks I often use the book as an example for this concept of edges. With physical books you can touch the object, you can literally feel those edges. There are certain affordances to the object itself because of its edges, and you know what you are getting into. With digital books and magazines, especially in the early years of that medium, navigation was happening on two axes – you could swipe left and right but also up and down. It felt unnecessarily complicated and really jarring with regard to having a sense of where you were in the experience. You were penalised for navigating somewhere else and leaving that linear space. If you wanted to jump to page eighty and you were on page thirty, good luck ever getting back to page thirty. Without clear edges we don't feel like we're in control.

As more and more virtual experiences enter our lives, do you think this need for edges will increase? Is the current craze for vinyl, printed books, and artisanal crafts more generally a reaction to the lack of edges in the digital space?

Absolutely! Whether people acknowledge it consciously or not, it's this return to quietude, to focus, to having something we can put our hands around and understand in totality. And I think that's really wonderful.

You can't and never will be able to understand Twitter. Every time we dip into it, it feels like you are dipping into a mosh pit of intellectual horror and joy and excitement and sadness. If you live in that world – which a lot of us do for many hours of the day – you suddenly want to spend a lot of money on a beautiful axe and go outside to chop down a tree. At least you understand the parameters of what you are doing. Or if you want to make bread, guess what? You can totally learn everything there is to know about making a simple loaf of bread. You understand what you opted into in a way that so much of the online world doesn't allow you to.

It even applies to building websites. Many of us feel a sense of responsibility to continue a web project forever. I think more web stuff should just end. You can put an end date on it. I was reading an article by a publishing industry woman yesterday on a popular blog that existed from around 2005 to 2012. One day she put a post up saying, 'So this is the last one! I'm going to keep up an archive. The comments are closed. Enjoy!' That's beautiful. I love that! It's important to recognise that that's OK to do online.

I think it can be quite damaging psychologically to the people who create things online if they feel like they have to be stewards of their creations forever. It's no surprise that we seek more and more physical objects and offline activities – things with edges – to avoid the kind of hopelessness that we get in the digital space.

While you're based in Japan, you still spend quite a bit of time in the US. What is one thing you enjoy most about each country that you miss when you are not there?

For me personally, America is basically three locations: New York City, the Bay Area, and Asheville in North Carolina. Generally, I love the ambition and risk-taking attitude of Americans. I go to New York for the people and the conversations. You can't have the same conversations anywhere else in the world. It feels international, holistic, and inspiring. When I'm in the Bay Area, talking to researchers and those venture capitalists who are more focused on longer-term investments, there is a sense of aspiration that's hard to find in any other place. People there work on problems at global scales.

Because of the way companies are structured,

there is a lot less so-called disruptive thinking in Japan, and as result there is a lot less risk-taking embedded into its startup culture. Part of the reason for that is the respect for craftsmanship I mentioned earlier. But unlike in the US, that role of craftsmanship goes beyond hipsterism.

Before you become a *shokunin*, which is a craftsperson, you're a *deshi*, an apprentice. Let's say you want to make pickles. You can't just start making pickles. You first have to go through your five years of pickle training before you can make your own pickles.

I love that, and not in an 'oh, that's so cute' kind of way. I love that as a life philosophy: you have to learn from people who know better than you, who have been doing it for a while. Sure, you can do something more interesting or disruptive, but you first have to understand the origins of what you're trying to change. This philosophy is embedded in everything here. It's wonderful.

What I also like about Japan is this sense of pervasive empathy. That empathy results in the national healthcare system and investments in infrastructure. Everyday I experience where my tax dollars go when I'm in Japan. Whenever I ride my bike I feel the smoothness of well-maintained roads. Take even, for instance, the state-run workout centres: each time I go to the gym, I pay two dollars. That's it. No membership fees. No bullshit contracts. Two bucks gives me this great gym experience, and I know I'm paying part of it in the background through taxes. Anyone in the neighbourhood – whether they pay a lot of taxes or a little – has access to this great, affordable gym. I think that's not only pretty cool, but of critical importance. ●

One of the greatest dangers to any creative project is allowing the potential for the thing to subvert your ability to make it, because you want to live in a world of potentiality for as long as possible. A book is always greatest before it's written. You are intoxicated by what it can be. That's very dangerous. You want to kill those seductions as quickly as possible, and one way to achieve that is fast iteration.

Craig Mod

A Day With
Khaled Islam Bouya

Khaled is a user interface and
experience designer working
from Boumerdes, Algeria.

7:30am It takes my alarm four to five snoozes to bring me back into real life. I indulge in the habit of replying to some messages and scrolling through Instagram before hopping out of bed.

7:50am I work from home, so I've made a short morning walk my daily exercise routine. It's a great way to catch up on podcasts too. Today it's Layout.

8:20am For breakfast I favour proteins: a couple of eggs, some luncheon meat, bread, and a cup of tea.

9:10am With another cup of tea in hand, I head over to my workspace. First order of business: a quick conference call with my project manager to discuss the most pressing to-dos of the day.

9:40am A project we've been wireframing for a while is finally moving into the design stage. Time to dive into Sketch to refine our ideas. Seeing the creative input of our team come into existence like that is one of my favourite things.

10:50am We usually build mobile apps based on Appcelerator Titanium. Since I don't know all the ins and outs of this framework, I regularly jump on a call with Redouane, our technical lead, to verify the feasibility of an idea.

1:05pm I go for a midday walk to pick up some ingredients from a grocery store nearby. Today's lunch: a barquette with bread topped with tuna, cheese, fried eggs, and some chickpeas.

2:10pm In another call with my project manager, we go over a list of feedback a client has provided. To avoid miscommunication and to make feedback cycles efficient I try to be included in most calls with clients.

2:45pm I start tackling feedback. The client wants to see how their app renders in tablet format. For some inspiration I browse Dribbble and Behance, and research articles on scaling up mobile designs.

3:35pm Time for a little breather. Twitter is my go-to place for keeping up with the design community, even though it sometimes feels like a breeding ground for negativity. Today is a perfect example, as I have to slog through the cynical reactions to Dropbox's recent rebrand in order to find some thoughtful articles I can add to my reading list.

5:20pm Before clocking out I push all the updates to InVision, a collaborative design tool our team and our clients love since we're scattered across France and Algeria.

5:35pm To clear the day from my mind I jump on my bike and cruise around town while enjoying some relaxing tunes, currently Lush Vibes.

7:00pm Some friends and I decide to take a forty-five minute drive to the capital, Algiers, to try a new pizza place we've heard a lot about.

11:55pm My good intentions for an early night are usually ruined by wallowing in social media or catching up on my reading list. ●

A Day With
Berglind Ósk Bergsdóttir

Berglind is a software developer for digital product studio Kolibri, based in Reykjavík, Iceland.

7:30am I enjoy getting up early for some quiet time. It still amazes me how fifteen minutes of yoga followed by simple meditation helps calibrate my body and mind for the day ahead.

8:00am I have breakfast with my eleven-year-old son Adam and help him get ready for school.

8:45am From door to door, it only takes me fifteen minutes on my bicycle to get to work. It's such a nice privilege to be able to ride to the office.

9:00am Three days a week I work out of our client's office; the other two days I work from Kolibri HQ, like today. Before I catch up on my emails and Slack messages, I head to the coffee station and make myself an oat milk cappuccino.

10:00am Time for our daily Slack meeting with the rest of the team currently working from our client's office. We are working on a big release of the Icelandair website. Lots of boxes to be ticked before the big reveal!

10:15am Settling in to get some coding done. I try to avoid multitasking so I can get in the zone for the rest of the day.

12:00pm I join my boyfriend Michael – also working at Kolibri, but as a designer – to get take-away food from Local, this amazing salad bar across the street. Before we get back to work, it's time for another pick-me-up: our ritual after-lunch pour-over coffee.

12:45pm Our weekly check-in meeting with the other Kolibrians brings us up to speed on how everyone is feeling about their work progress and, perhaps more importantly, we discuss personal matters – our joys and struggles.

1:30pm While I'm certainly not a fan of meetings, I feel it's important to work not only *in* but also *on* the business. That's why we've organised an internal retro(spective) meeting to reflect on our relationships with our clients.

2:00pm I finally finish a tricky development task. These things always take longer than expected, don't they? While I'm waiting for a code review on GitHub, I throw some darts to clear my head.

5:15pm Back at home, I cook a traditional Icelandic dish called *soðin ýsa:* boiled haddock and potatoes, mashed with butter, and some fresh vegetables on the side. It tastes better than it sounds, I promise!

6:30pm Adam and I play a card game, then cozy up on the sofa and watch a couple of Modern Family episodes together.

9:30pm After putting Adam to bed, I catch up with Michael over FaceTime.

10:00pm I'm working on my book on impostor syndrome, which is based on a talk that I've been giving at conferences around the world. The tranquility of the night helps with writing.

11:00pm A few pages of *The Sirens of Titan* by Kurt Vonnegut help me clear my thoughts and get ready for bed. ●

As chief design officer at Melbourne-based digital agency Today, Adam oversees the design of products and services that generate positive social and environmental impact.

The Ethical Agency
Adam Morris

Most designers and technologists I know share a similar disposition: they're curious, restless, optimistic beasts who love fixing stuff. The more broken, the more challenging, the better. They also find it hard to sit around and be spectators while the world around us is falling apart. Yes, we've made a lot of progress, but there is still so much to be done.

To that end, at Today we spend our time working through complex social and environmental problems. We feel a deep sense of obligation to use the things we're good at as levers for change.

Defining 'good work' can be tricky. It's important to have a foundation for discussion and debate around new work opportunities. We rely on the UN's publicly available Sustainable Development Goals as part of these discussions. It's a ready-made framework that defines seventeen key areas to focus on. Keeping those goals in mind makes it easier to have robust conversations about projects that we do or don't take on.

Of course, certain industries we just flat-out refuse to work with. 'Good' companies not only maximise value for people and planet – they minimise harm to them. Ruling out industries like tobacco, fast food, and gaming comes easy. As a purpose-based business, we're defined as much by the clients we say 'no' to as those we say 'yes' to.

As a team, we regularly discuss what 'impact' means on an individual level and then we try to connect people with those fields they feel most strongly about. This makes for better work and happier people, and so, naturally, it's good for the business as a whole.

Being crystal clear about our values also helps with our hiring process. It's pretty rare that people kick in the door trying hard to get a job if they are apathetic about what we stand for.

Just like at any other agency, it can be a hard slog at times. But the more we grow and the more we can see the positive impact our work has, the more rewarding it feels. Success for us is proving the case that doing 'good' is good business. We want to inspire people to go out and have a crack at it, just like we did.

To effect change in a meaningful way, we now know that we need to play an active and loud role in fighting for action over inaction. The world needs big, new, unconventional ideas over safe, marginal tweaks to broken systems. As a bunch of designers and technologists, this is where we are at our best: unlocking new ideas from within affected communities, co-designing better solutions, challenging bureaucratic, old behaviours, and providing a vision for a better way forward.

Based in Sheffield, UK, Nicola co-founded digital studio Yoomee with her partner Andy out of her love for the charity sector, after many years as a researcher and an information, publications, and policy specialist.

Nicola Mayer

More than thirteen years ago, Yoomee was born of necessity after my husband's shiny job in Denmark burst with the dot-com bubble. I quit my job at a national charity and we combined our skill sets to become Yoomee, an agency that reflects our personal values and seeks to make the world a better place through the innovative digital products we develop. Both of us had enough experience to know the sort of place we wanted to create – the kind we'd always aspired to work in, but had never really experienced. So we set about creating our perfect jobs and finding clients and employees who shared our desire to see social justice made real.

In the mid-2000s, focusing on such a niche sector seemed like a massive punt. Yet, from the beginning, charities admired and embraced our unique set of values, user-centred approach, and desire to see the digital medium amplify their reach and impact.

We start every relationship by stating that we only work with organisations with social purpose at their core – period. We then approach our work through a set of values we've refined over the years. These include impact over profit (don't chase the money); show, don't just tell (have a strong bias towards action); and be real (we're human).

Potential clients are sometimes surprised to learn that we select them with as much care

as they select us. We want long-lasting relationships built on mutual trust and respect. Mostly this happens by natural selection. We don't have to explain away why we sometimes say 'no', because we are very candid about Yoomee's narrow focus on social impact work.

In hiring, we choose personality and commitment to our social values over any technical skill set because skills are relatively easy to attain. Putting an emphasis on human qualities benefits our clients and enriches the quality of our work. We're all aware that, ultimately, our work is much more about people than technology. If you don't have the humility and empathy to put yourself in the shoes of your clients and their customers, you're going nowhere!

Looking back over more than a decade of Yoomee, sadly, we've learned that non-profits often lag behind in understanding how innovation in the digital space can really benefit them. Therefore, our role is a hand-holding one: helping non-profits to interpret their world through a digital lens.

Lately, we've also seen the funding for digital innovation getting harder to come by. Organisations are growing risk-averse. However, we remain optimistic that scarcer funding means more, rather than less, innovation, through small projects with big impact, powered by passion and hope for positive change. ●

The trailblazing social
entrepreneur continues
to reinvent herself
in life after Kiva.

Jessica
Jackley

INTERVIEW
Kai Brach

PHOTOGRAPHY
Shayan Asgharnia

When Kiva launched in 2005, online crowd-funding was in its infancy. Since then, this not-for-profit microfinance platform has provided over a billion dollars in tiny loans to entrepreneurs in underdeveloped regions of the world. After exiting Kiva several years ago, co-founder Jessica Jackley looks back at the turbulent early days of a social enter-prise with a truly global impact. Humble, content, and energised to do still more, she reflects on her career in philanthropy, inspired by the stories of entrepreneurial farmers, seamstresses, and goatherds.

Was there a particular moment when you realised that philanthropy was what you wanted to pursue as a career?

When I graduated from college, two things directed my path. First, I dreamed of working for a great non-profit. I assumed that's where I had to spend my waking hours in order to work on something I truly believed in. Second, I was dating someone who lived in California, so I moved to Palo Alto to live down the street from him. I was completely without a plan or prospects. It's funny to look back at that time and realise that these two driving forces really didn't give me any career direction. They did, however, lead me to relocate to the Bay Area, where I experienced very different opportunities and a different culture full of entrepreneurial thinking.

A few days after I had moved, I found myself in this temporary administrative role at the Stanford Graduate School of Business. It wasn't a bad job by any stretch, but it wasn't my dream job. While I was there, I got close to all these amazingly driven people graduating and going on to start non-profits or social enterprises that created lasting impact. I wanted to do what they were doing! And I was pretty sure that meant I had to make some changes.

I started to do a lot more active observing and interviewing. I crashed lectures, sat in on conferences and other events, and did whatever else I could do to understand how these people around me were using business skills and entrepreneurial thinking to address social problems. One night, I attended a lecture by Dr. Muhammad Yunus, a Bangladeshi social entrepreneur who would later go on to win a Nobel Peace Prize for his work on microfinance. His story really resonated with me. The fact that a tiny amount of money at the right time in the right person's hands could be a complete game changer – it was just astounding to me.

A few weeks later I quit my job at Stanford and I begged my way into an internship with a non-profit called Village Enterprise. At the time, it was giving people in East Africa one-hundred-dollar grants to start or grow small businesses. I wanted an excuse to spend time with these people, learn about their lives, and, hopefully, be a good enough listener to do something helpful for them. So for three months I travelled through rural Kenya, Uganda, and Tanzania to interview grant recipients. And it was then and there that I learned some of my first and most powerful lessons about entrepreneurship – not from Silicon Valley titans, but from farmers, seamstresses, and goatherds.

What specifically inspired you about Dr. Yunus' talk? The microfinance model was relatively new but surely not unheard of at that time…

Hearing how Dr. Yunus' story had started was a huge source of inspiration to me. Instead of just thinking about poverty from afar, he got up close and personal with people, sitting down with them and listening carefully to their stories. He heard about people's struggles directly, from their own mouths, and then responded to *those* needs – not some preconception of what they might need. I remember thinking, 'Well, if his great work started with being a good listener, maybe mine can too. I can be a good listener. I can go out there, listen really carefully to the people I want to serve, and act on that.' It may sound naïve, but I really believed it was going to be the best strategy for me. It felt like the right way to figure out how to be helpful in the world.

Dr. Yunus managed to talk about those living in poverty in a way that didn't seem to have an agenda of scaring me or guilting me. He spoke of people who were poor, but who – of course – were just people, not projects to be solved or casualties to be saved. They had dreams and aspirations in life just like anyone else, but unfortunately didn't have access to opportunity. They were simply dealt a different set of resources, services, and communities than us.

His approach freed me from a cycle I'd been stuck in for a long time, where well-intentioned non-profits would tell a story of poverty with the sole intention of evoking guilt or shame or panic so that you'd give money at the end. Dr. Yunus told stories of empowerment as well as struggle, potential as well as need. It was a more balanced story, and one that gave me

a glimpse at a role I could play myself – not just as a guilty far-off donor responding to a sad story, but maybe as a participant or partner relating to another human being.

When you arrived in East Africa, what was the first-hand experience of poverty like for you?

I think a lot of us who live in relative privilege are taught from a young age that people living in poverty are in need of material goods – food, clothing, shelter – and that it is our job to provide those for them. We're constantly exposed to images of sadness and suffering and hopelessness, and as a result we develop

that kind of predictable response I mentioned earlier: we feel sad, guilty, even shameful. And yes, poverty is something to feel sad about, for sure. And I do believe that every one of us who has relative privilege is absolutely obligated to help. But every human being has a multi-faceted story, and I think it's dangerous to hear only the sad side of that story, because eventually we just stop listening – or at least I did, for a while.

Anyway, during that trip to East Africa, I tried to remember what had inspired me about Dr. Yunus' talk and all the reflecting I'd done since. I made a conscious effort to just interact with people without too many assumptions or expectations about their lives. I tried to go into conversations with an attitude of openness

and graciousness and not 'here I am to swoop in and save the day!' And of course, I heard about lots of challenges and difficulties, but also about triumphs and resourcefulness.

It was after returning from that trip that the very first version of Kiva was conceived. This was long before the concept of crowdfunding was widely understood. What problems did you run into at the beginning?

It's so strange to think back to that time. No one was using the word 'crowdfunding'. We were stumbling over our own long-winded explanations when telling others about our idea. And there was a lot of pushback. People didn't quite understand how such an idea would work technically, nor why anyone would participate in it.

There were lots of practical concerns and questions around the technology. Was there even internet in Uganda? How would you move the money around? How could you trust people or establish a system to keep everyone in check? Admittedly our plan was risky, but we felt that we'd found good ways of mitigating that risk.

By far the biggest unknown was whether anyone would be interested in lending small amounts of money to strangers halfway around the world – let alone doing it for free! To be honest, on paper it didn't make a lot of sense: why would anyone lend money without receiving interest on that loan or getting any tax-deductible benefits from it? At that point we just hoped that we could find enough people who were willing to chip in $25 or $50 or more out of sheer goodwill. Of

course, this wasn't a donation but a loan. If all went well, the money was returned to them.

All of those questions felt very real and daunting back in 2004. I think that's why it took me and my co-founder, Matt, a whole year to create the initial version of Kiva. It took us a year to gain enough confidence to try something so new and unproven. For months, we were shopping around for feedback and looking for someone to give us a big 'thumbs up' or encouragement that we weren't living in some sort of utopian dream. Of course, there's no one out there who gives you permission to go try your idea out. At some point you just have to trust yourself and jump.

And it took off faster than expected. What do you think was the reason for its popularity? Was it good old marketing or was it an intrinsic feel-good factor that made people excited about sharing their Kiva experience?

I think it was a nice convergence of lots of different things. Timing was one of them. Microfinance was trending and we were the first to try out zero-percent loans through this unique crowdfunding style.

We were also lucky in getting a lot of buzz in the blogosphere. We made it onto some of the most popular blogs then, including Boing Boing and Daily Kos. Suddenly, we had this onslaught of attention and traffic from the right people who were just a click away from transacting.

Then the more traditional media followed and every few months we'd get some other media hit that would propel us to the next level. One year in, we were part of a PBS Frontline/World special report; the following year we were featured on Oprah, alongside Bill Clinton. It's was surreal. In the background we were white-knuckling it and hanging on for dear life, trying to keep up with these crazy spikes of traffic.

But more than anything, I think – or I'd like to think – that it was the stories we shared about our borrowers that just clicked with people. Lots of people found themselves in the stories we shared on Kiva: a detail in a borrower's life story would resonate with them. For instance, maybe a mother of three kids would lend to another mother of three – a seamstress trying to build a business to create enough income to feed her three daughters. Maybe a person went on vacation somewhere near the place where a farmer was trying to raise money for a new generator. We definitely didn't anticipate the myriad of person-to-person connections that could be made through the borrowers' profiles on the website.

All in all, to be honest, the correct answer to why Kiva turned out to be so successful is that we happened to be doing enough things right and not too many things wrong. It was an idea whose time had come, and we happened to be there. We were imperfect stewards of that idea, but we tried our best, showed up everyday, and thankfully that was enough.

And what a phenomenal success it is! I believe that earlier this year Kiva celebrated *one billion dollars* in loans. Amazing! Do you think lending is a more powerful charitable tool than just donating money?

Current location
Los Angeles, CA, USA

Hometown
Pittsburgh, PA, USA

Top bookmarks
gmail.com, amazon.com, twitter.com, wsj.com, nytimes.com

Top apps
I'm anti-phone lately, staying present with the humans around me. I often don't carry it with me or I just use it as a phone.

Recommended reading
God: À Human History by Reza Aslan, *Rocket Fantastic: Poems* by Gabrielle Calvocoressi, *When The Moon Is Up* by Students of Alain Leroy Locke High School

Inspired by
My three sons, who are six (twins) and two, drop these little insights every day that just stop me in my tracks. Like most children, they observe without emotional baggage, or fear, or an agenda. Usually, the stories they tell themselves about the world are radically optimistic. They assume the very best in people again and again, and challenge anyone who won't.

Favourite accessory
A print by Los Angeles artist Rob Reynolds that reads in big, bold capital letters, 'NOTE TO SELF; BE KIND, BE KIND; BE KIND.' It reminds me to have an intention of gentleness, within and beyond myself.

Tea or coffee
Coffee. Pour-over. No more than two cups per day is my rule.

On the web
jessicajackley.com
kiva.org

I wouldn't say lending is more powerful in an absolute way. I'd say that it has interesting qualities that make it more attractive to some people.

By its nature, lending has the potential to be stickier than donating. In a donor-beneficiary situation, the donor gives money to an organisation and the transaction is complete. Maybe there's a nice follow-up – a thank-you note or something of the sort – but that's it. A loan, however, is never just a one-way transaction; it's an exchange. It's a back-and-forth of money, information, and gratitude. It helps build a unique kind of relationship – a dialogue that promotes mutual respect and a sense of optimism.

Imagine you see a person begging on the street. And now imagine you see another person who is eager to tell you about their business idea, about how they want to be more productive, and how they get up early every day to work hard for a better future. For most of us, it's easier to imagine carrying on a longer, deeper conversation with the latter person. Obviously, I am not suggesting we should ignore someone begging for money. I do think, though, that Kiva helped reframe people's stories in a way that drew others in.

It's a similar perspective on the receiving end. Whenever I've had the chance to interview Kiva borrowers, they reiterated the following in one way or another: when given the choice between receiving just a loan – say, from a local bank – or receiving a loan from a community of people who know your story and are cheering you on from near and far, almost everyone chooses the latter. For entrepreneurs, the encouragement from and the accountability to a global community of supporters – in addition to funding – is a much more powerful combination.

Having met so many entrepreneurs in under-developed countries, what are some unique lessons you've learned about the entrepreneurial spirit of people who have so little?

As you know, I wrote an entire book about this question! At its centre is the notion that entrepreneurship is much more than just starting a venture. It is a way of living, a way of going through your days identifying problems and responding to those problems creatively and resourcefully.

One definition of entrepreneurship that I call on a lot when I'm teaching is Howard Stevenson's. He described it as 'the pursuit of opportunity without regard to resources currently controlled'. What really speaks to me is this spirit of going over, around, and through obstacles, no matter what. It's about pushing forward with dogged determination to realise a vision not only when circumstances are perfect, but *despite* the lack of resources.

Importantly, as I interpret it, 'resources currently controlled' doesn't just have to refer to funding. It means anything else that an entrepreneur may think they need to move ahead. It could be an actual, tangible resource or the lack of an idea that is holding you back. Or it could be a naysayer, a barrier, a burden, or a reason not to take that next required step.

What I learned through Kiva is that for people who are incredibly disadvantaged, entrepreneurship can be this beautiful, redemptive, life-giving call to action *without having to wait for things to be perfect.* Many of them could easily list a thousand valid reasons why they may not succeed, but I have met so many individuals who go ahead and pursue their idea anyway. True, this is often out of pure necessity – in many cases it's a life or death situation – but I don't think that makes the choice any less courageous. Hearing their stories taught me that entrepreneurship is first and foremost about resourcefulness: how to push forward in an environment of scarcity.

For those living in poverty, money seems to be a means to an end. In our society, accumulating more money has become the ultimate end. Can we still apply the same definition of entrepreneurship?

No one should be criticised for where they were born and what they have or don't have. Having said that, it's very easy for those born into a well-resourced place to live in a bubble of wealth and privilege. Consequently, what they may conclude are worthy problems to solve may not be relevant to other people, maybe even to the majority of people on the planet.

Many choose to spend their workdays building things that will, at best, make life a little bit easier for those who already have a pretty easy life. That's fine; that's their prerogative. They may be motivated by building *something* – anything at all. I can relate to that. Or they may want to make as much money as possible, as fast as possible.

I believe we can have the best of all worlds: working on projects that solve crucial problems for huge segments of people, while still getting that rush that comes from building and creating every day, *and* getting you and your team paid well.

I do think there are different types of entrepreneurs and different ways of practicing entrepreneurship, of course. Some people become entrepreneurs to survive. A lot of others – myself included – get to pick whether they want to be an entrepreneur and how they want to go about it. This group can choose to build virtually anything they dream up. Obviously, I wish more of them dreamt about, say, making faster progress toward fulfilling the United Nation's Sustainable Development Goals, and fewer cared about hacking their way to yet another mobile app.

So the tech community carries a particular responsibility?

Well, in the startup culture emanating from Silicon Valley we see this very masculine push to grow as fast and as big as you can. It presumes that value can only be derived from massive financial gain. Even in the social sector, where there might be different incentives, there is now an assumed notion that something is not worth doing unless it can scale quickly and become sustainable.

So many people play along with this self-perpetuating culture without taking a moment to reflect on what they're building, and why, and what the end goals are. How intimidating is entrepreneurship if we just look at it through this lens of infinite growth? It's paralysing, and unfortunately I think it short-circuits a lot of otherwise valuable ideas and ways to serve people on – God forbid – a smaller scale.

It's important to remember that there are things worth doing that will absolutely never become financially successful or even sustainable. It doesn't mean those endeavours are less important or that the people running them aren't investing enough time, money, or effort.

I realise I'm speaking about this as someone who has started a venture that *has* scaled and has the potential to be sustainable. It's been a wonderful thing to watch unfold. But I believe Kiva could've only started with small, specific experiments, one person at a time. It wasn't scalable or sustainable in the beginning. Even if it hadn't grown and scaled as tremendously as it has, I think it still would have been worth doing.

How has your relationship with money changed over the years and what can the borrowers that you've met teach us about the value of money?

In the year we launched Kiva, I made a total of under ten thousand dollars. The only reason why I was able to survive and work on Kiva was that my co-founder – and partner at the time – had a full-time job. Money was pretty tight but I couldn't have cared less. I was incredibly happy.

Fifteen years later – after finishing business school, after leaving Kiva, and after many other ventures, jobs, and projects – I'm more confident in my ability to create value and I understand how I can capture some of that value for myself. In other words, I know how I can get paid for the work I want to do. And I don't think there's anything wrong with making sure your own needs are met. It's not wrong to want to make a healthy living while trying to save the world.

Today, my relationship with money actually feels much less like a relationship because there is so much less emotion involved than there used to be. I am lucky enough to be comfortable, but I also feel less excited or motivated by money than ever. It's so clear now that money is just a tool to get somewhere. It's a means to an end. I've always known this, but over time, I've come to feel it too. It's freeing.

As for what I've learned from Kiva borrowers: money may be an obvious way to get what you need, but it is rarely the only way. I think it's healthy and useful to have a bit of scepticism, to pause and ask if there is another way that helps you move forward.

In what ways are running a non-profit organisation different from running a for-profit business?

Well, first off, there are many organisational structures to choose from and the one that makes it easiest to reach your goal is the one you should choose. After all, your structure is just a tax code, not a religion, and while there are restrictions around each of them, you have a lot of room for creativity.

As a for-profit, you may be able to find the best seed funding, for example. That's great. And although its main goal is profitability, the structure may still end up doing a lot of good in the world. On the flip side, some organisations will reach their goals fastest as a non-profit because they can source a major asset pro bono, for instance.

Either way, you can build a strong culture with a passionate team in any structure, especially if you are clear about your values and stay committed to them. Sure, it can be a great motivator to be able to offer your team actual equity in a company or provide performance-based bonuses, but it's also possible to create a sense of ownership without handing out shares. It's a wonderful fact that a lot of people who are drawn to non-profits are motivated by things beyond a big paycheck. That motivation is a powerful tool and advantage for organisations in the non-profit sector.

I think it's worth mentioning that non-profits don't operate on a different set of business rules or practices. Many non-profits often still strive for 'profitability'. They just use different language to talk about it – they call it sustainability. However, a non-profit *has to* commit to reinvesting the money it generates back into the organisation rather than paying it out to executives or investors. I think most businesses have a lot to learn from non-profits, especially around casting big visions, motivating employees through things other than money, and thinking about their impact beyond just delivering a product or service to a paying customer.

How has the decision to run Kiva as a non-profit impacted you personally?

There is a weird danger that's kind of unique to people working in the social sector: you tend to get too wrapped up in the idea that your work is your identity, your complete and total reason for existing. Since your sense of purpose is so closely tied to the good things you're trying to achieve, it's very easy to become a complete workaholic. The deeper your belief in your goal, the more of a trap it can become. As

a society I think we over-glorify the sacrifices people make to contribute to good causes. In other words, if you're a business person who is overworked, people usually tell you to take a break. If you're doing social impact work, no matter how overworked you seem, people just high-five you for doing the right thing.

There is another, more practical aspect of running a non-profit that's rarely discussed: an 'exit' looks very different. In a for-profit, there are clear and obvious paths for the business, often leading to a sale, an IPO, or a partner buying you out if you want to exit the business. There is no such thing in the non-profit world. If a founder decides to leave – like I did with Kiva a few years in – there is no actual 'cashing out'. I left a startup that I had invested a big chunk of my life in and the next day I was out there looking for a job to pay my rent. It may be hard to believe, but I truly don't have any regrets. I've been rewarded in so many other ways from that work, and I would do it all again in a heartbeat.

As an aside, something I've discussed with other people who started their careers launching a successful non-profit: if, later, you become interested in going on to work in a more traditional company in the for-profit

sector, people can be quick to judge that and question whether or not you're suddenly a sell-out. It's so strange. Being a wildly successful business person first, who then has a change of heart and starts a social enterprise later in life, often earns a lot of respect and recognition. Doing the reverse is harder.

Why did you decide to leave Kiva around 2009? How difficult was it to move on?

One reason for leaving Kiva was that I was going through a divorce with my then-husband and co-founder. We both realised that working together at the same office was no longer an option. But besides that, I felt that I had successfully proven that I could build something meaningful and valuable. I was ready to move on and create something else. I didn't want to be just 'that person who created Kiva'.

Leaving wasn't easy. Going through that season in my life was a double loss of identity: personally, because I was going through a divorce, and professionally, because I was leaving the organisation I had founded.

I remember catching up with a friend and asking her with tears in my eyes, "What if I never get to do something as great as Kiva?" And her sobering answer was, "Well, let's assume you won't. It was great and now it's done. OK. So now what do you want to do?" Her bluntness gave me the jolt I needed and forced me to dream bigger than work, to think about all the other things I wanted to do in my life.

Today, my work is a combination of many parts and projects, some paid, some unpaid. I teach, I write, I consult, I parent. But everything I do stems from my values, and I do my best to integrate all of the lessons I've learned, across projects and roles. It's shocking to me how many hard-earned lessons from my entrepreneurial ventures apply to parenting and how things I learn from teaching apply in the boardroom.

Today, the idea of 'making the world a better place' has become a mantra for everyone in tech. How do we choose a problem that really needs our attention and how do we define the impact we can have?

First off all, I applaud anyone who takes the time to reflect and name what really matters to them. But often people miss a crucial step: prioritisation. For example, my work matters a lot to me. So does my family. So does my health. So do my friendships. So does my volunteer work. They *all* matter to me. What's important is to figure out how to place what matters *most* at the top and put the rest of them in a specific order from there. I think the same principle applies when we look at progress versus problems in the world. Choose the issues that matter most to you, then contribute. A little bit of participation is all it takes.

Every person gets to define impact for herself. The kinds of impact I think matter most fall into two categories, and they are placed on extreme ends of a spectrum. On one end, there's alleviating suffering, starting with meeting the most basic needs we all have. Impact at this end of the spectrum is visible. It's visceral and it's easy to measure. I value that *so* much. On the other end, there's the invisible, difficult-if-not-impossible-to-measure kind of impact. Here, I value showing love, inspiring hope,

encouraging those who are discouraged, and in general helping people believe that more is possible for themselves and for others.

My goal is to make contributions that have real, visible effects on meeting basic needs, and hopefully, at the same time, to leave people feeling loved and full of hope.

You're also a mother of three young boys. Beyond the obvious ones, is there a certain quality or an understanding that you learned throughout your entrepreneurial life that you want to pass on to them?

I want my boys to believe – *really* believe at a gut level – that every person on this planet is important. I want them to be able to stand strong in what they know to be true, but at the same time to have soft hearts and the ability to listen well. I want them to believe that they have a responsibility to dream big – bigger than any generation has before them, maybe. Mostly, I want to leave a legacy of love for them, to fill them up with so much love that it overflows to others as they go through life. ●

It's important to remember that there are things worth doing that will absolutely never become financially successful or even sustainable. It doesn't mean those endeavours are less important or that the people running them aren't investing enough time, money, or effort.

Jessica Jackley

Rules of Business
Aarron Walter

Aarron is the VP of Design Education at InVision and founded the UX practice at MailChimp. His design guidance has helped The White House, the US Department of State, and dozens of major corporations, startups, and venture capitalist firms.

Be willing to adapt.
On average, people have three careers in their lifetime. Chances are that what you're doing in ten years will be very different from what you're doing now. Be open to change, to new roles in your organisation, or an entirely new career. If it's a scary change, then you're probably heading in the right direction.

Hire people, not skills.
Think about all the people you've known who were let go – maybe *you* were let go. Most of the time it's a lack of soft skills that lead to termination. When you hire, focus on traits like social aptitude, humility, and adaptability. These are things that are hard to coach, and that if absent will lead to chaos in a team.

Speak their language.
Designers often struggle to speak the language of business when communicating with engineers and executives. Stay out of the weeds. Talking about grids and type treatments won't draw people into your cause or your vision. Talk about your work in terms of business goals and how the customer experience is affected in order to help non-designers understand your work.

Guard your time jealously.
If you're not careful, your colleagues and clients will steal your time one Google Calendar invitation at a time. Block off periods on your calendar for deep work that requires your full attention. When it's time to be productive, kill your internet connection and the onslaught of notifications that steal your time.

Gain mastery by teaching others.
I've found that I never truly gain mastery of a process or concept until I teach others how to do it. Teaching requires reflection on your process and careful consideration of the importance of each step. That's why I build writing and public speaking into my work, so I can continue to grow.

You are not your work.
Your passion for your work can trick you into thinking that your work is your identity. That's dangerous. What happens when you no longer do that work? You may wonder who you really are. You are more than your work: you have more to contribute to the world. Build your identity around things beyond your professional life. ●

Numbers in Perspective

721 million

Number of internet users in China.

51.8%

Percentage of total internet traffic generated by bots, not humans.

269 billion

Total number of business and consumer emails sent and received per day globally.

50%

Percentage of new businesses that survive their first five years, according to the US Bureau of Labor Statistics.

A internetlivestats.com
B census.gov
C incapsula.com
D distilnetworks.com
E radicati.com
F statista.com
G bls.gov
H –

326 million

Total population of the USA.

96%

Percentage of websites with login pages that were hit by 'bad bots'.

59.8%

Percentage of total email traffic classified as spam.

90%

Percentage of startups failing in their first year according to unidentifiable sources, repeatedly shared online.

Our Sponsors

We take pride in working with companies that understand the value of unobtrusive sponsorships and a great reader experience.

hover

With the countless hours you have
devoted to your passion, your hard work
deserves a great domain name. Hover
is where the internet's best ideas get
named. No gimmicks. No upsells. Just
easy domain and email management.

Save 15% by visiting hover.com/offscreen

ueno.

We have a question.

What's the best advice anyone
has ever given you?

Something that changed your life for the
better. Maybe a lot, maybe just a little.
Something that made you think, 'I wish
somebody had told me that before.'

We'd like to know what it was. Then
we'd like to pass it on to the people
who read our blog. We're all in this
together, and maybe one day your
advice will help someone else out.

ueno.co/goodadvice

balsamiq®

What is most important for
your work on the web?

[ ] Reliability and performance you can count on
[ ] Creative freedom to build whatever you like
[ ] Ownership of your web content and data
[ ] Easy access to a wide range of tools

At SiteGround we check all the boxes.
We specialise in web hosting for open-
source applications that let you keep
control over your content, get crafty
with your design, and move freely
between platforms. We also believe
in supporting open and independent
publishing online *and* offline.

If this is the kind of web you want to
be part of, join us and get 50% off at:
siteground.com/offscreen

Adobe Typekit

When you read, what voice do you hear in your head?

Look up from this magazine for a moment. Read the nearest printed word or sentence. Then look back here. How does *that* voice compare to *this* one?

This text is set in Acumin, a typeface designed by Robert Slimbach. It's one of the thousands available on Adobe Typekit, a subscription library for fonts.

Whether your work ends up on the web, on stickers, or on bookshelves, Typekit is the best way to get the fonts you need for all your creative projects – with no need to worry about licensing.

If you're already an Adobe Creative Cloud member, full library access is included with most subscriptions. Or check out purchasing options on Typekit Marketplace, which uses the same font sync and web hosting technology to deliver an even broader range of type, with prices set by participating foundries.

So what voice will *you* try next? Start exploring on typekit.com

MailChimp

Whether you're looking to up your
email game, sell your stuff, or find your
people, we've got tools that give you
the confidence to grow your company
in a way that feels right for you.

You went out of your way to try the new café downtown. You made it to that off-the-beaten-track ramen spot in Tokyo. Now log it all so you don't forget where you've been. Lifelogging with Swarm allows you to have a memory bank of your movements, so you can share your favourites with friends, reminisce about good times past, and gain new perspective into who you are.

Your journey through life is uniquely yours. Check in and remember everywhere: swarmapp.com

HARVEST

Tuesday, 02 February

Time	Task	Notes
06:00am 06:12am	Waking up	OK, campers, rise and shine!
06:40am 06:42am	Coffee	Slept like a baby. Love some coffee.
06:45am 06:48am	Chit-chat	Ran into (and away from) an old acquaintance.
07:13am 07:38am	Taping	Covering an ugly little rat.
07:42am 08:57am	Breakfast	Tip-top of the morning to you.
09:17am 09:19am	Saving people	A 'thank you' would be nice.
10:00am 12:00pm	Piano lesson	A little Rachmaninoff...
01:34pm 03:19pm	Learning French	Memorising Baudelaire.
04:59pm 05:24pm	Seducing Rita	A drink to world peace.
08:10pm 10:14pm	Evening dance	Some jazz piano to close out the evening.

Adobe Typekit
Balsamiq
Harvest
Hover
MailChimp
SiteGround
Swarm
Ueno

WORDS
Alice Default
Ivana McConnell
Kai Brach

Gear
Office Objects

1 →

A smartwatch with classic appeal
This watch hides its smarts well: the
Nokia Steel is a smartwatch with a classic
watch design. Your daily activity progress
is elegantly and unobtrusively displayed
on an analogue subdial. The watch also
tracks your sleeping patterns and wakes
you with gentle vibrations. Our favourite
feature: eight months of battery life.
health.nokia.com

2 ←

Charging cable and battery in one
You're already carrying around a
charging cable, so why not attach a
small battery pack? Nomad's Battery
Cable combines a durable, ballistic
nylon, braided, MFi-approved Lightning
cable with a high-capacity 2350-mAh
portable battery. And it knows your
priorities: it charges your phone first
before charging its internal battery.
hellonomad.com

3 →
Stand better

Finally got a standing desk to ease your back pain, but now you're struggling with sore feet? The Topo Mat is here to help: the patent-pending surface design encourages frequent movement and engages the blood-pumping mechanism of your calves. With a cushioning, supportive material, Topo promises more movement, more blood flow, and a healthier you.
ergodriven.com

4 ←
Your keyboard-to-go

Logitech's Keys-To-Go is an ultra-portable, standalone keyboard for your tablet or phone. Dirt and water resistant, with a battery that lasts up to three months, this bluetooth keyboard is just six milimetres thick – you'll barely notice you're carrying it.
logitech.com

5 →
Wireless charging

Pi introduces wireless charging: a patented power platform changes the angle of a magnetic field to perfectly match the angle of your device. It can charge up to four phones at full speed, or even more devices at reduced speed (even if they're moving) in close proximity to the Pi station. And it follows existing FCC safety guidelines. The result is safe, seamless power.
picharging.com

6 ←
Combat-ready backpack
Originally designed for special forces soldiers going into combat, the GR1 Rucksack comes with extra-padded straps and handles, silent zippers, and a hydration port. Its durable, rainproof material is able to carry up to 180kg of contents, in case you decide to bring that extra-large battery pack. The GR1 has you covered, whether you're taking part in a survival camp or just trying to keep your laptop safe during your morning commute.
goruck.com

7 →
Present with confidence
To be a confident presenter you need a reliable remote for your slideshow. Spotlight's minimalist design hides a lot of very neat features, including a pointer for controlling the on-screen cursor without touching your laptop, customisable vibration alerts to keep you on track, and three hours of battery life after a quick one-minute charge.
logitech.com

8 ←
Monitor desk shelf
The Grovemade Desk Shelf provides an ergonomic lift and ample space for up to two screens, and is crafted from 15-ply premium maple plywood, aluminum, and natural cork. It's designed to last a lifetime and is suited to almost any modern work configuration, providing subtle organisation for your space.
grovemade.com

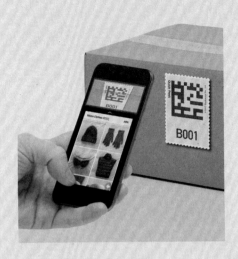

9 ←
Take stock like a pro
Quick Peek are self-adhesive smart labels that work with a free companion app to help you keep track of your stuff. Stick a label to your box, snap some photos of its contents, assign a location, and Quick Peek will do the rest. Wherever you store it, you'll always know what's inside every box. You can even sync the details via iCloud or Dropbox and share with your family or team.
bluelounge.com

10 →
Get a grip (on your phone)
With ever-growing screen sizes, holding your phone securely is getting increasingly difficult. Ungrip belongs to a new category of products designed to help avoid a costly drop. This lightweight sling – available in many colour combinations – attaches to the back of your phone and offers lots of different ways to hold it securely.
ungripyourphone.com

11 ←
See-through ruler
The Glass Ruler by Areaware is not just a beautiful desk accessory that will become the envy of your colleagues – it's a practical tool that helps you measure in centimetres or inches without getting in the way.
areaware.com

12 ←
A pen as mighty as the sword
Made by knifemaker Böker, the CID Cal .45 Tactical Pen is not only a handy writing device, but also a CNC-milled titanium bit of personal protection. Use the integrated pocket clip to keep it on you at all times, and, if a dangerous situation ever arises, it doubles as a strong blunt object. The bolt action also makes for an addictively fun way to click it open when you're scribbling notes.
bokerusa.com

13 →
The customisable wifi ticker
The LaMetric is a wifi-connected programmable pixel display, bluetooth speaker, and alarm clock in one. Use the accompanying mobile app to decide how you want to use it: show your Facebook likes in real time, get email notifications, or let it display the weather forecast or the latest stock quotes. The possibilities are endless.
lametric.com

14 ←
Beautiful, wireless sound
You'd be forgiven for thinking it's jewellery. The Beoplay E8 are beautifully presented, high-performance, wireless headphones. The case doubles as a charging station on the go and will give you two additional charges. E8 is tuned by the same audio engineers that tune all other Bang & Olufsen products, so expect exceptional sound quality. The E8 comes with the Beoplay App, giving you full control over the characteristics of your sound and allowing you to define presets for different sound scenarios.
beoplay.com

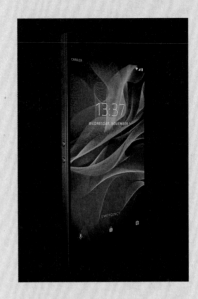

15 →

A phone for gamers

The Razer Phone is a new Android-powered phone optimised for mobile gaming. With an impressive display with higher-than-usual refresh rates and an extra wide colour gamut, front-firing speakers and dual amplifiers, a Qualcomm Snapdragon processor fine-tuned for maximum performance, and one of the largest battery capacities found in any smartphone to date, the Razer Phone sure packs a punch. razerzone.com

16 ←

Technology that hurts us

Many of the digital services we rely on are full of oversights, biases, and ethical nightmares. Chatbots that harass women. Social media sites that send peppy messages about dead relatives. Unfairly weighted algorithms that put more black people behind bars. In her book *Technically Wrong*, Sara Wachter-Boettcher takes an unflinching look at the values, processes, and assumptions that lead to these and other problems. amazon.com

17 →

Programmable keyboard

If you want to get really geeky about keyboards, Kono has you covered. Their latest product, the WhiteFox, is a compact keyboard, optimised for rapid typing and signal delivery to your computer. With a large range of superior mechanical switches and keycaps, it's a keyboard in a new class of its own – fully program-mable and open source to the core. kono.store

18 ←
Recycled chair
The Pod PET Felt is a privacy chair for breakout areas in offices. The material used is unique in that it's not just sound-dampening to increase the sensation of privacy within crowded spaces – it's also made of recycled PET bottles, and as such the chair itself is recyclable too. The design of the Pod chair allows a number of production steps to be reduced to one smart 3D pressing technique. Don't like the shape of this chair? There is a whole range of PET chair designs and materials available. devorm.nl

19 →
Pocket phone
Fox Mobiles makes phones so small you won't be tempted to do anything else with them but call or text. The Fox mini 1 works as a standalone phone, or you can pair and synchronise it with your smartphone over bluetooth, so you can stash the latter away and still get your important calls and messages. The size of a credit card, this minimalist phone is a great backup for tight budgets, or for all of us trying to spend less time tapping, posting, and scrolling. foxmobiles.com

20 ←
Secure authentication
Enterprise-level security for everyone: trusted by companies like Facebook and Google for their employees' credentials, the YubiKey is a USB key that makes two-factor authentication fast and easy. Just touch the key when connected to your computer or tap it against your NFC-enabled Android phone to complete authentication on all of your favourite websites and services. yubico.com

21 ←

Gadgets, deconstructed

Exhibiting the insides of old and new technologies, photographer Todd McLellan lays bare everyday items and displays them in mesmerising detail. From Macintosh computers to old typewriters, breaking down the complexity of the gadgets we take for granted reveals the engineering and design mastery contained within. Todd's work is available as a book or as prints for your wall.
toddmclellan.com

22 →

Open-source 3D printing

The latest version of the popular, upgradable 3D printer from Josef Průša is as versatile as its predecessors, but packs in more features. It handles a huge variety of materials, from Nylon to Bamboofill, and ASA to Polycarbonates. All of its parts are open-sourced, meaning you can make suggestions for improvements. Buy it pre-assembled and pre-calibrated or (cheaper) as a kit to build yourself.
prusa3d.com

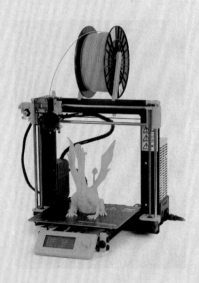

23 ←

Multi-dimensional sound

Love the surround-sound experience at a movie theatre? The Ossic X is able to accurately render spatialised stereo through a set of headphones. By pairing advanced 3D-audio algorithms with head-tracking and individual anatomy calibration, the Ossic X delivers accurate 3D sound – increasing the sense of auditory space. ●
ossic.com

Aral
Balkan

The human rights
activist who believes
Silicon Valley is telling
us billion-dollar lies.

INTERVIEW
Kai Brach

PHOTOGRAPHY
Kamila Schneltser Pinilla

Aral Balkan is not shy about voicing his opinions on Silicon Valley. He believes America's tech giants run a digital panopticon that enslaves and farms the world's population. The designer, entrepreneur, and self-proclaimed 'cyborg rights activist' travels the world to spread a powerful and alarming message: in order to defend our human rights and democratic principles, we need to rise up against the algorithms that are filling the pockets of venture capitalists. Under his small Malmö, Sweden-based organisation, Ind.ie, Aral shares critical thoughts and develops alternative products that offer a more egalitarian, sustainable vision for the future of technology.

One does not wake up one morning wanting to become an internet activist. What led you to dedicate your time to activism?

My first experience with digital technology dates back to the era of personal computing. I was 7 and I started making games for myself in BASIC. It was a purely hedonistic pursuit. Later, when I started making apps for others, I realised what a profound impact these tools could have on their lives. I began to understand the crucial role of design. There was this sense of excitement that we could use computers to create impactful and delightful tools that would empower people and improve their lives. I also remember when I first came across software that would sneakily record what you were doing and then leak that information to third parties. Back then, we called it 'spyware'. What I didn't realise was that, with the advent of the World Wide Web, this would become the dominant business model of mainstream technology.

The web era has ushered in a social system that Soshana Zuboff from Harvard Business School calls 'surveillance capitalism'. It's the result of a feedback loop between surveillance, the accumulation of information, with capitalism, the accumulation of wealth. In this system, already-wealthy individuals use venture capital to subsidise businesses that help them extract and accumulate intimate information about all of us, which is then used to amass yet more wealth by exploiting us. This feedback loop has resulted in a world where the richest five men have as much wealth as the poorest half of the world population combined, according

to a study by Oxfam. That's 3.5 billion people! Who are these five men? Familiar names from the tech world: Mark Zuckerberg, Bill Gates, Jeff Bezos, Larry Ellison, and Michael Bloomberg.

As I gradually became aware of how surveillance capitalism works, I made a decision to no longer contribute to perpetuating this system. Edward Snowden's revelations were the last straw. That's when I decided to dedicate myself to not just raising awareness about the issue, but to start creating a compelling counter-narrative.

The last four years have been a long learning process, but I think we're finally making some progress. Here in Europe, at least, there is far more of an understanding of the problem and we're starting to see legislation like the General Data Protection Regulation (GDPR) and the upcoming ePrivacy Regulation that aim to tackle some of the issues of these toxic business models.

You call yourself a 'cyborg rights activist'. When I hear the word 'cyborg' I tend to think of RoboCop, not my fellow web citizens. Whose rights are you trying to protect?

If you use modern technologies today, you are a cyborg. When I choose to store a thought, experience, or idea not (just) in my biological brain but on my smartphone, I'm extending my mind and thereby extending my *self* through this device. It makes sense

to broaden our understanding of the boundaries of the self beyond our biological limits to
include these technologies as mere extensions
of our selves. When we do this, it becomes
clear we don't need a special set of 'digital
rights' or 'data rights.' Instead, we must apply
the human rights we already have to this
extended understanding of the cyborg self.

If my phone is an organ – just like my
brain – that stores my thoughts, governments
or corporations have no right to access it,
unless I give them permission to do so. Most
of our 'digital organs' are not implants. They
are – like our phones – *explants*, but they
are no less a part of ourselves. Surveillance,
under this model, is an abuse of the self.

Adopting the concept of the cyborg self is
a prerequisite for protecting the integrity of
personhood in the digital age. Without it, we
cannot guarantee that we – as individuals – will
have ownership and control of ourselves.

It's also crucial to specify what we mean
when we talk about 'data', because this word
is meaningless without a qualifier. Do we
mean data about objects or about people?
It's a crucial distinction that we often fail
to make in the debate about Big Data,
especially when it comes to giving permission to corporations or governments.

With the right data, I can hurt people –
emotionally and physically. As a government, I can deprive a person of their
freedom or even of their life. You can't do
any of that to objects. That's why data about
objects should belong to the public – the
commons – but data about people should
belong to the individuals themselves.

**Why aren't more people concerned
about their privacy? Is the issue too
abstract or does the convenience of
the tools we use just make us lazy?**

I don't think people are lazy. They are being
lied to with billion-dollar budgets. When Google
and Facebook market their products, they don't
tell you how exactly they make money. Their
algorithms are not on display for you to see, so
you don't know how they are processing your
data and what conclusions they derive about you.

According to what it says on its homepage,
'Facebook helps you connect and share with the
people in your life.' Next to this tagline there is
an image of a decentralised network in which
people are connected directly to one another.
This is false advertising. Facebook doesn't
connect us to one another, it connects all of us
to Facebook, Inc. The company is the man in
the middle who gets to track, store, analyse, and
exploit all of our interactions. While Facebook
likes to portray itself as a public space, it's very
much a private space. It's a shopping mall but
it wants us to think of it as a park. The problem
is that a shopping mall is private property. You

can use it for. Of course, regulation is just one part of the equation. We must also create viable alternatives that are funded and designed ethically.

What constitutes a more ethical approach to creating software? Can we make existing software more ethical?

It's actually not about the software; it's about the business model. Once a corporation has proven 'successful' through an unethical business model, it's impossible to ever change that business model. Google and Facebook are hugely successful by current economic measures, so why would they be interested in changing their ways? Even with mounting pressure, the best they can do is to make their products appear less threatening. In other words, they work hard to decorate them superficially so that their need for data about you doesn't feel creepy.

That said, not every company has the same business model. Especially in Europe, there are still lots of companies that sell products, not people. Of course, Silicon Valley is quick to ridicule them by calling them old-fashioned. But we don't even have to travel to Europe to find an alternative business model.

don't have a right to free speech or to privacy in a mall. The only rights you have are the ones that the owner of the mall grants you. You can be tracked, censored, or ejected at any time.

And it's not just Facebook. All of our digital spaces today are privately owned and heavily commercialised. We talk a lot about the web democratising industries and removing gatekeepers, but in reality we've lost the public sphere – with dire ramifications for our human rights, and chilling effects for democracy.

To make people aware of what's actually happening with their privacy, we must regulate these corporations to force them to label their products properly. Beyond labelling, we must also limit what data they can gather, how long they can store it for, and what purposes they

Apple, for instance, makes the majority of its money selling products. When you buy an iPhone, Tim Cook is happy. He doesn't care whether you use it or not because the company already made its profit the moment you purchased the device. Of course, he'd like you better if you also buy a few apps from the App Store and movies from iTunes, but even then, Apple's profit is based on selling you things instead of selling *you*. Google, on the other hand, starts making money not when you buy an Android phone but when you start using it. For Google, customers are only valuable when they can start farming them.

Once you understand this difference, you realise what a massive competitive advantage privacy can be. For Apple, privacy is an *absolute* competitive advantage. It's a feature that Google cannot provide without choking off its main source of income. In other words, if Google made its products respect your privacy, they would go bankrupt. All they can do is compete on the *illusion* of privacy. That's why Apple is investing huge sums of time and money into building artificial intelligence and other features in a way that respects privacy. It's the only absolute competitive advantage they have over Google.

Other companies should be asking themselves whether they want to follow the Google model or the Apple model. When some of the regulations I mentioned earlier come into effect in Europe, companies with business models based on farming you for data are going to incur huge administrative costs. They will have to limit how much data they gather and what they can do with it. Companies that build decentralised, zero-knowledge systems, on the other hand, won't have the same restrictions. They'll be free to innovate. That's privacy as a competitive advantage.

The notion of 'people farming' through deceitful design is a recurring concept in many of your talks. Can you explain what exactly you mean by that?

At its core is the now well-known fact that companies like Facebook and Google cater to two audiences: their users and their customers. Fittingly named, 'users' are the people they must get addicted to their products in order to gather the insights that are monetised through their customers – advertisers and

other interested parties. Those other parties, for example, include Cambridge Analytica – a company that used Facebook data to influence the outcome of Brexit in the UK and the presidential elections in the US. The more time you spend using their systems, the better these companies can profile you and then exploit that information for their own gain.

By the way, even if you don't use their products, they still gather data about you. A common practice is to purchase information about you from data brokers. They even get data from governments. The city of Amsterdam, for example, shares all of its citizens' licence plate information with Google in exchange for a 'free' app that helps people find available parking spaces. This is hugely shortsighted, of course. Governments must learn a cardinal kindergarten rule if they want to protect the privacy and rights of their citizens: never accept candy from strangers. Or, more specifically, never accept candy from Silicon Valley.

Anyway, in order to distract from an extractive and exploitative business model, Google and Facebook practice decoration, although they prefer to call it 'design'. Design is about creating useful, empowering tools that improve our lives. Design is *not* about masking the acrid smell and the bitter taste of a toxic business model by adding 'convenient' features and crafting an addictive experience around it. That's *decoration*. The goal of decoration is to create a beautiful, tasty, poisoned apple: it looks great, it tastes wonderful, and it is detrimental to your wellbeing.

Decorating for addiction – I refuse to call such a toxic practice 'design', as I'd like to reclaim that word – is a core feature of Silicon Valley products. It is inextricably linked to the business model loved by venture capitalists. Their bible is a book called *Hooked: How to Build Habit Forming Products* by Nir Eyal. Note that Nir's book is not a 1984-esque warning, it's an instruction manual. In Silicon Valley, addiction is not a bad word: it's the means by which you ensure that your livestock keep using your machines while you farm them for maximum value.

You also make the case that these same companies prevent us from having a truly decentralised web infrastructure. How so?

Before personal computers, there were mainframe computers. These were someone else's computers. They were owned and controlled by large corporations and educational institutions. You had to rent time on them. There was no expectation of privacy and you could only use them for the purposes that the owners of the machines permitted. The personal computing era decentralised and democratised that. You owned and controlled your PC. You had the right to choose what you kept to yourself and what you shared with others. In other words, you had privacy. And no one told you what you could or could not do with your own property. That all changed when the World Wide Web became mainstream. The web has a client/server architecture, a centralised architecture. The servers are the centres. In the early days, there were many centres, relatively speaking. So we mistook it for a

decentralised system. But when we injected venture capital into that system, the existing centres were incentivised to grow as rapidly as possible. And grow they did. They grew and coalesced – through mergers and acquisitions – until just a few monopolies remained.

Thomas Watson, president of IBM for much of the twentieth century, famously said, "I think there is a world market for maybe five computers." He was almost right. He was just off by one generation of technology. The five computers we have today – our modern mainframes – are Google, Facebook, Snap, Amazon, and Microsoft. So, really, the web era is the Mainframe 2.0 era. Or as the Free Software Foundation likes to say, 'There is no cloud, just other people's computers.'

By the way, IBM's Watson super-computer is named after that same Watson. Italy just sold the full medical histories of all of its citizens for use by IBM Watson in exchange for $150 million. For historical context, the original Mr. Watson received a special medal from Hitler to honour extraordinary service by a foreigner to the Third Reich. More recently, IBM's current president wrote an open letter to president Donald Trump with suggestions for ways they can work together. I feel the combination of these facts should, at the very least, give us all reason to pause.

What would the alternative to an internet run by corporations look like?

The alternative is an internet run by people. Imagine an internet where every person owns and controls their own place – a personal node that all of your 'smart things' connect to. You don't have to set up or maintain this space

yourself: it's an interoperable service that's hosted by lots of different organisations to avoid lock-in. This is a free and open system so you don't have to put your trust in any one of these providers. The underlying code is open, which means you can verify it and even run it yourself if you have the necessary technical knowledge.

Looking back, we've moved from mainframes to personal computers to the web. It's the swing of a pendulum from centralised to decentralised and then back to centralised. My efforts as an activist focus on giving that pendulum a good push forward towards the next decentralised era of technology: the personal networking era.

There are a lot of challenges ahead. One of the most difficult ones is that a lot of infrastructure has already been built under capitalist success criteria. Those criteria, of course, are very shortsighted. Take the domain name system, for example. One of the key elements of an effective decentralised system is for everyone to have their own, easily accessible identifier, like a domain name. Unfortunately, domain names are currently sold in a marketplace based on artificial scarcity and can take anywhere from five minutes to many hours to activate. To get an identifier from Facebook – that is, one they allow you to rent in exchange for the right to profile you – you only have to fill out one very simple form, which takes you thirty seconds. Getting your own decentralised website up and running involves finding a domain registrar, buying a domain name, waiting for it to propagate, getting a server, installing the software to run your website, et cetera. And you need to know how to do all of that in the first place.

So, one of the greatest design challenges to take us into the next era of computing will be to enable everyone to have a *decentralised* presence within thirty seconds. I'm confident we can do it, but we may have to find a way around the current domain name marketplace.

I assume such a network would be financed with government help. Our governments are not exactly known for being fast innovators. If not through the capitalist system, then how do we incentivise innovation given how much of the technological change we're going through at the moment is fueled by the prospect of massive financial rewards?

It's worth noting that a system that's funded by taxes is not the same as a system built and run by the government. The latter will not work for the reason you just mentioned. I've heard some people calling for Facebook and Google to be nationalised. That's the last thing we should do. We must regulate them to limit their abuse while replacing them by funding ethical alternatives from the commons. What we definitely don't want is governments having direct access and control – even more than they do now – over these centralised surveillance devices. So, we must regulate and replace.

We can incentivise this effort from the commons by investing our tax money to subsidise lean not-for-profit organisations that take what we know works from startups – small teams, iterative development, and so on – and throw out the toxic element: private venture capital. Instead of celebrating and idolising start-ups, we should be supporting and investing in stay-ups. And eventually, we must go beyond private equity subsidy and push governments to invest in what is essentially our new public infrastructure. I don't see this happening in the US any time soon, but there is great potential here in Europe.

Given the lobbying efforts by big corporations and the willingness of local governments to accept funding for public projects, what can be done to realise your vision?

Big corporations are allowed to spend millions to influence public policy-making and stave off regulations that could limit their reach. Big Data follows the Big Tobacco playbook. A few short years ago Google wasn't involved in lobbying. Today, they're the largest lobbier of the European Commission. Initially, they got away with most of us not grasping the dangers – just like it was at the peak of cigarette sales. Remember that doctors once appeared in tobacco ads!

Now that policy makers are catching on to the dangers of people farming, the likes of Google are trying to influence legislation through financial means. Former Google executive Eric Schmidt once told me, "I get

Current location
Malmö, Sweden

Hometown
Ankara, Turkey

Top bookmarks
better.fyi, source.ind.ie,
forum.ind.ie, mastodon.ar.al,
duckduckgo.com

Top apps
Better Blocker, Amaroq,
Encrypt.me, Signal

Recommended reading
Accessibility for Everyone
by Laura Kalbag, *White
Hat UX* by Trine Falbe,
The Social Contract by
Jean-Jacques Rousseau

Inspired by
Edward Snowden. Not
only did he make sacri-
fices for what he thought
was right, he's also a
humble, compassionate,
and lovely human being.

Favourite accessory
My Nabaztag bunny with
one pink ear and one cyan
ear. A decade ago, it spoke
out the comments left on
my blog. Although it's inac-
tive now, it's still adorable to
look at and I keep it on my
desk as it makes me smile.

Tea or coffee
I love both, but there is a
special place in my heart
for a cup of Turkish coffee
with plenty of sugar.

On the web
ar.al
ind.ie

up every morning and I fight regulation. It's
what I do. It's my job." They are certainly not
ambiguous about their goals or methods.

But it's not just lobbying – 'revolving doors'
are an issue too. If a member of the European
Commission who is responsible for protecting
the privacy of European citizens can take on a
role at Google two years later, that's corruption –
plain and simple. We often think about corruption as a 'money under the table' thing, but it's
this kind of *institutional* corruption that is much
more powerful because it is currently legal.

So a crucial first step towards regu-
lating these giant monopolies is to
remove the corruptive influence of corporate finance on public policymaking.

**You're obviously not shy about using
dystopian imagery to get your message
across. Do you think a certain level of
alarmism is necessary to wake people up?**

We don't need dystopian imagery to get our message across. Simple, accessible, factual explanations of the business model of mainstream technology are more than enough. The analogies I use are not alarmist. They're descriptive. I'm doing nothing more complicated in my analyses than following the money. We must realise that we are not sleepwalking into a dystopia: *we are already there*. The sooner we realise that, the sooner we can start working on alternative – fairer, kinder, more sustainable – paths forward.

I mentioned the parallels between Big Tobacco and Big Data earlier. We're slowly starting to see the sentiment turn against Big Data as the practices of big corporations become more and more socially unacceptable. Just as today no 'star graduate' would want to work for Philip Morris as their first choice of job, in a few years we're going to see developers and designers shunning Facebook and Google. From the chat I had with Eric Schmidt I also remember him saying, "If we ever become too evil, we won't be able to find anyone who wants to work for us." Just a few weeks ago, someone messaged me to let me know that they had turned down a job offer from Google because they did not want to support a people-farming operation.

So our efforts right now are focused on creating the counter-narrative and viable alternatives. I don't plan on being an activist for life. Hopefully, in the not-too-distant future, what I'm doing now won't be necessary and I can go back to just making things – like I was doing in the personal computing era – but this time in a networked, decentralised world.

You previously tried to develop various products under the Ind.ie label that didn't materialise, like the Ind.ie Phone. What did you learn from those failed undertakings? Is resistance to these giant corporations futile, or were your ideas just ahead of their time?

Ind.ie is a non-profit that we set up to truly understand surveillance capitalism and to encourage alternatives to it. As such, the only failure would be if we were to stop working on possible solutions before the problem is solved. That said, it takes a bit of experimentation to figure out the most effective approach.

We abandoned the idea of a phone when we realised that it was not feasible to create both a decentralised ecosystem and a product as complex as a phone all at once. Without a decentralised infrastructure in place, we would only have built yet another device that would connect to the same centralised services.

As we continue to better understand the problem, we concentrate on areas with maximum impact. To finance our initial experiments, I decided to sell a family home in Turkey. We then had a crowdfunding effort and raised $100,000 to build a prototype of a decentralised messaging system, which we did. To finance the development of Better, our tracker blocker, I again dipped into my own savings. Sales of Better now help us pay the rent, but it's not enough to keep us sustainable. That's why at the moment we rely on a combination of those sales and my own speaking fees to keep us going.

This year, we have an exciting opportunity to work with the Belgian city of Ghent and its 260,000 citizens to implement what could be the beginning of the 'Internet of People.' We'll be working quietly on that for a while. So I'm excited about 2018.

Working on a large-scale problem like this with a small team is difficult at times, especially since we're trying very hard to make sure we don't compromise our integrity in any way. Not taking money from large corporations makes paying the rent a bit harder.

There's a lot of talk about a post-capitalist future. Looking beyond just the tech sector, what large societal shifts are necessary to create enough momentum for people to see an alternative to the status quo that isn't immediately dismissed as 'too idealistic'?

A lack of imagination makes us see realism that deviates from our everyday experience as idealism. Especially in the US, where capitalist thinking is so deeply ingrained in every aspect of society, a different way of life seems completely unimaginable.

Meanwhile, it's becoming clearer every day that capitalism isn't sustainable. No system built on the core assumption that we can have infinite growth with limited resources is. When the cells in our bodies forget their role in the greater organism and start to grow uncontrollably and selfishly, we call it cancer. Why do we model our success criteria on the success criteria of cancer? And, if we do, how do we escape its endgame? The only answer capitalism seems to have is that technology will somehow – magically – save us.

The question isn't whether a post-capitalistic future is realistic. The question is 'how much are we willing to make ourselves suffer before adopting a more sustainable and fairer model?' Am I optimistic? No. It's possible that we've already passed a point of no return, but I hope not. I remain realistic – with imagination.

More practically speaking, in what ways can I be a more ethical web citizen without completely shutting myself out of most of the internet?

That's easy: support companies that sell products, not people. This often means paying for things. For example, instead of Google Mail, get a paid Fastmail account. Instead of Google Drive, use Basecamp. And make sure you tell those companies why you chose them so that they know privacy matters to you.

Beyond that, there are also many decentralised, free, and open tools available. Try Mastodon as a Twitter alternative. A company called Purism is offering laptops and soon phones that respect your privacy. If you have the technical knowledge, help out your friends and family by assisting them with moving away from centralised, surveillance-based silos.

If you *really* want to get involved, take on the design challenge I presented earlier: create a decentralised communication system where getting up and running with your own node takes less than thirty seconds. The first system that manages this with a semantically extensible messaging format will have a shot at becoming the next web.

Many of us have friends working for some of the big corporations you're going up against. Is it fair to criticise all of them for their decision to work there or does that judgment require a bit more nuance?

We all come across situations in life that we don't necessarily agree with but which we're benefiting from – whether intentionally or not. That's when we have an important decision to make: do we choose moral principles or short-term financial gain? Although it doesn't seem that way at first, both choices are actually pretty selfish ones, because it comes down to this simple question: what kind of world do we want to help create? The world we help create will be the one that we have to live in ourselves.

Also, it's important to acknowledge that these data-hungry monopolies don't just lie to their users, they also lie to their employees. A lot of people go to work at Google and Facebook believing they're making the world a better place. That's why raising awareness about their business model is essential. Once you fully understand the system you're a part of, that's when you have a decision to make: do I keep doing this because of a six-figure salary and stock options? Or do I quit because it goes against my principles, and this is not the world I want to help build and live in?

By the way, even if you're not feeling the ramifications of surveillance capitalism today, it doesn't mean that you won't in the future. If you're a gay person living in San Francisco, you probably don't see the danger in sharing your sexual orientation on Facebook. That can't be said of a person who lives in a country where being gay is punishable by prison or death. As a middle-aged white person living in the West, it's more likely that you will first encounter surveillance capitalism in a more subtle form: perhaps your insurance premium will go up because your smart fridge is sharing data about your unhealthy eating habits.

We don't need charities to fix this. We just need a shift from extremely shortsighted selfishness to enlightened self-interest. What does the world you want to live in look like? It probably doesn't look like the feudalistic mess of patriarchy, surveillance, and extreme inequality that Silicon Valley promotes. So, use your privilege – if you have it – to create a world in which you wouldn't need it to begin with. •

Design is about creating useful, empowering tools that improve our lives. Design is *not* about masking the acrid smell and the bitter taste of a toxic business model by adding 'convenient' features and crafting an addictive experience around it. That's *decoration*. The goal of decoration is to create a beautiful, tasty, poisoned apple: it looks great, it tastes wonderful, and it is detrimental to your wellbeing.

Aral Balkan

WORDS
Sean McGeady

Profile
Ecosia

Sowing
the Seeds

Christian Kroll is a man with a lot of weight on his shoulders – the weight of one billion trees, to be exact. He is the founder of Ecosia, a Berlin-based social business and search engine that uses its profits to support tree-planting programmes all over the globe. The company was created in 2009 after Christian embarked on a round-the-world journey of discovery. Since then, its business model has been revised, and it has tangled with Google, flirted with Yahoo, and partnered with Microsoft, all leading up to a landmark moment: in 2014, after five years of strife and growth, Ecosia planted its one millionth tree. Christian responded not with backslapping and complacency, but with the lofty ambition to plant one billion trees by the year 2020.

The native of Germany was always enterprising: he was trading stocks by the age of 16. But Ecosia represents Christian's biggest undertaking to date – tackling the existential threat to our civilisation that is climate change. If we are to combat this rapidly worsening problem, we'll need to make effective use of the natural processes we often seem so intent on destroying. That's where Ecosia comes in.

A mature tree can absorb more than twenty kilograms of carbon dioxide (CO_2) in a year, and an acre of trees can produce enough oxygen for eighteen people to breathe over that same period. Given that the United Nations' World Meteorological Organisation recently announced that the level of human CO_2 emissions in our atmosphere has reached its highest level in 800,000 years, the planet needs all the trees it can get. Beyond their chemical capabilities, trees also form habitats and provide food for billions of birds and insects, and can help restore landscapes and restart water cycles. Ecological advantages aside, forest goods, such as fruits, nuts, oils, and sugar can provide dependable income sources for farmers in less developed countries, resulting in less regional migration and reducing the chances of civil conflict.

The old expression says 'money doesn't grow on trees', but for Ecosia, the opposite is true. Like Google, Yahoo, and most other search engines, Ecosia's search results feature ads. When a user clicks on an ad, Ecosia is paid by the advertiser and that money goes directly to putting trees in the ground. The social business then donates eighty percent of the profits from its search-ad revenue to nonprofit conservation organisations for financing reforestation projects in countries such as Brazil, Burkina Faso, and Indonesia.

The breadth of Ecosia's endeavours has it working in communities all around the world and, by trading knowledge between different countries like Tanzania and Morocco, the startup has been able to cut its expenses and increase the efficiency of its tree planting. Today it costs Ecosia €0.22 to plant a tree. Its numbers are all publicly available, published in the company's monthly financial reports. The hope is that by being transparent about where Ecosia's profits go, any sceptics will be drawn to the cause. All you really need to know, however, is that by using Ecosia instead of Google – you can install the Ecosia extension on your preferred browser – you can make a difference in the fight against one of the world's biggest challenges.

Ecosia keeps you updated on the difference you're making too. A counter on its homepage informs users how many searches they've made. On average, every forty-five Ecosia searches results in enough ad revenue to plant one tree. Christian's own counter stands at more than 7,000, which means that his searches have led to the planting of about 155 trees, but, given that he's the brains behind the enterprise, it might be more accurate to say he's had a hand in the planting of more than sixteen million.

Over the past year, Ecosia's growth has been remarkable. Until late 2016, it took the company between six and nine months to plant one million trees. Today the thirty-strong startup plants about 1.5 million trees every month. By the end of the year it will have planted twenty million trees – about seventy-five per cent of those in 2017 alone. But it wasn't always this easy. Ecosia's roots stretch around the world and its trajectory has been shaped by both failures and epiphanies.

Christian was several years into a business administration degree at the University of Erlangen-Nürnberg when he realised that his values didn't align with those of his tutors and peers. He was being taught that businesses exist to produce and optimise profit. But he had other ideas: 'Who says that a business' existence has to be defined by profit?' With that quandary in mind, he knew he had to finish his course as quickly as possible or

stop studying altogether. He did the former – but mainly to keep his parents happy. Freed from the shackles of education and the idea of profit-based business, Christian was free to ponder his next move. But before he could find an opportunity, opportunity found him. "Around this time a friend asked if I wanted to go to Nepal," says Christian. "I'd been travelling before and had experienced what it's like to live in poorer countries, but this felt different."

It was on the rocky slopes of the Himalayas that Christian came to another profound realisation. "I knew that I wanted to do something good with my life, but I didn't have a great understanding of what 'good' actually meant," he says. "Then I realised how many opportunities I had compared to the people of Nepal, who were more motivated than I was but didn't have the same freedoms as me because I'm from the West." Struck by a sense of global injustice, Christian created Xabbel, a search engine whose profits would go directly to financing NGO projects for the Nepalese.

A smart idea, you might think. Christian disagrees. "In hindsight it was stupid," he says. "The internet market in Nepal was so underdeveloped that it was really difficult to make money. Even Google was losing money in Nepal." Xabbel worked but it didn't take off. The future founder of Ecosia had another decision to make: should he stay or should he go? This time, fate forced his hand. With an around-the-world plane ticket in his pocket and its expiry date fast approaching, Christian had to double down or admit defeat. Xabbel wouldn't last

much longer. But the seed had been planted.

From here Christian travelled the world until he ended up in Argentina, where Ecosia really took shape. Having toured the country and seen the harm that people can do to the environment, Christian found himself reading *The New York Times* columnist Thomas Friedman's *Hot, Flat and Crowded: Why We Need a Green Revolution – And How It Can Renew America*. "I liked it a lot," he says. "Friedman gives a good perspective on the issues we have and how they're connected to each other." In the book, Friedman states that seventeen per cent of global CO_2 emissions are caused by deforestation, which gave Christian his next idea – which also turned out to be somewhat naïve. "I thought, 'All we need to do is stop cutting down trees and we've almost solved the problem – that shouldn't be too hard.'"

Putting to use everything he'd learned in Nepal, Christian moved back to Germany, dusted off the search-engine idea, and created what would eventually become Ecosia – but not before another setback. Initially launched as Forestle in 2008, the project was running on Google's search results – until suddenly

Location
Berlin, Germany

Established
2009

Founder
Christian Kroll

Employee count
30

Business type
For-profit, B Corp

On the web
ecosia.org

it wasn't. "When I launched the project it got some attention from the press," says Christian. "But then Google walked away from it, which was a bit of a problem because a search engine without search results is useless."

Undeterred, Christian found another partner in Yahoo. "They were interested not necessarily because they're greener than Google," he says, "but because they're a competitor of Google – and a competitor with very little market share." Christian relaunched the company as Ecosia in December 2009. The plan had come to fruition. It was good timing too. Ecosia's relaunch coincided with the United Nations Climate Change Conference in Copenhagen, which saw the noble start-up attract a lot of attention – and its first few thousands users – as a result. But its business model hadn't yet been perfected. Christian's company may have been too noble for its own good.

The plan was always for Ecosia to donate as much as possible to the cause of planting trees and protecting forests. But Christian would soon see the other side of the coin: he was giving

so much away that he couldn't afford to pay his staff. "We were giving away about ninety per cent of our revenue," he says. "Everything that wasn't server costs or for my survival was given away. It wasn't sustainable. We had to make investments so that we could grow."

Ecosia revised its business model in 2015. Its policy today is to give away at least eighty per cent of its profits, which is around fifty per cent of its revenue. Aside from the money required to pay its employees and for future investments, everything goes to planting trees. "Whatever we don't need we give away," says Christian. Ecosia's refreshed approach changed everything. Suddenly the company had the money to promote the project, resulting in more media attention, which meant more users and more trees being planted. Ecosia's growth also meant that the company could finally put down proper roots of its own.

In 2015, after spending five years in a shared workspace, Ecosia finally moved into its own offices. Based in Berlin's trendy Kreuzberg district, Ecosia's headquarters are the kind of comfortable work-meets-play habitat typical of a twenty-first-century startup, complete with red-brick floor, exposed steel beams, recycled wooden features – and a rope swing. It was around this time that another significant shift took place. Impressed with Microsoft's commitment to innovation and user experience, Ecosia bid adieu to Yahoo and signed an exclusive contract with the Microsoft-backed service Bing, the world's second-biggest search engine.

As it previously did with Yahoo, Ecosia now gets one hundred per cent of its search results from Bing, and with that comes a degree of trepidation. If Microsoft were to suddenly end the partnership or its servers were to collapse, Ecosia would grind to a halt. "It's a tricky position," says Christian. "We don't want to be dependent on another company. We want to be more independent in the future." For now though, there are benefits to being in this perilous position. Christian's company may be dependent on Microsoft, but the tech giant is also dependent on Ecosia.

Bill Gates' multinational is a direct competitor of Google and is always working to chip away at the Californian behemoth's eighty-percent market share. Ecosia, and all the social good that comes with using it, is one of the few enticements that might cause users to wriggle free from Google's clutches and migrate to Microsoft's Bing. But beyond the cold, hard business at the core of what these companies do, Ecosia is also pushing for a greener agenda and has become a well-meaning thorn in Microsoft's side. "We always ask questions of them even though they're such a huge company. We're probably a very uncomfortable partner," says Christian, with more than a hint of pride. "We always ask about their CO_2 emissions and why they don't run on one-hundred-per-cent renewable energy yet."

Not just content with helping Microsoft, Christian wants to help Ecosia users go green too. But with the presence of Google looming large, it's not easy to branch out – even for a company whose purpose is to plant trees. "It's scary to have Google as a competitor," says

Founder Christian Kroll visiting one of Ecosia's reforestation projects.

Christian. "You'd better think twice about doing anything in this market because Google is so powerful." Nevertheless, Ecosia's developers are planning a system that will help users make more sustainable decisions while shopping or booking holidays. By rating search results according to their environmental impact, Ecosia will help users see the larger impact of their purchases. Looking for a new washing machine? Maybe there's a regional, seasonal, or second-hand option available. Booking a holiday? Perhaps you can reach your destination using an alternative route with a lower CO_2 footprint. Practically, the system would be small and unobtrusive for users, but the difficulty in developing it is one that Christian is intimately familiar with: money. "We have six developers at the moment," he says. "If we want to build something like this it's very resource-intensive. Google has 60,000 people working for them. If they wanted to build something like this it would be easy."

But before Ecosia can begin diversifying its offerings, it must first make improvements to its core service. Though they may be negligible, there are differences between using Ecosia and using Google or Bing. Among

other things, the German search engine lacks the smooth map, Wikipedia, and Oxford-dictionary integration of the US multinationals. Want to convert a currency? Ecosia can point you in the right direction but it can't make that calculation for you. Not yet anyway. It's this lack of certain single-click conveniences that proves to be a barrier for many.

If Ecosia is to reach its goal of planting one billion trees by 2020 it will need about two-per-cent global market share – and to reach that magic number it will need two-thousand-per-cent user growth. To attract and retain that many users, the search engine will have to be operating at maximum efficiency, ironing out bugs, and broadening its capabilities. Ecosia's first milestone was not easy to reach. It took the startup six years to plant its landmark one-millionth tree. If it is to reach its next milestone, Ecosia will need to pick up the pace. And what happens when they get there? We think Christian will probably waste little time in issuing another ridiculous noble ambition. One trillion trees by 2040? Make it happen, Christian – the world needs it. •

One Question
What career advice would you give your younger self?

Don't stay too long in your first job. Try out a few. Only then you will realise what you really love doing.
Bodo T.

Figure out what lifestyle you'd like to have, then build your career around it – not vice versa.
Nolan Kemp

Confront the things you know you're struggling with.
Kathrine N.

Do not confuse working hard with working long hours. Find ways to make your work meaningful and still be able to go out and enjoy life.
Nate

There is more potential to learn and grow from opinions you disagree with than from those you share with others.
Marcus

Don't sell out. Have strong moral principles that serve as your North Star. Find a job you can enjoy with confidence, knowing you're doing the right thing.
Shana F.

Take risks. There is always the safety net of friends and/or family.
Jason D.

Have an evolving bucket list of career goals. You can't know now what's worth achieving later in your life.
M. Dayley

Ask more, find a mentor, be confident. There are no experts, just people with a lot of practice and devotion to what they do. Find a way to make ideas happen. Experiment and take more risks. It's all hard work.
Ludvik Herrera

Don't buy into the busy bee buzz. Be a sloth. Remember, slow and steady wins the race.
Mel H.

Be the person in the room that speaks the least but makes every word count.
Carl Lonnberg

Forget what your parents told you about career choices. 'Professional development' is no longer a linear path. Take breaks and unforeseen detours to see where they take you.
Ruben Scheer

The most valuable skills in life cannot be learned through tutorials or textbooks, but through interacting with other people.
Jamie L.

A selection from 91 responses to our online questionnaire.

Use the first years of your career to experiment and find your niche. Rushing to jump the ladder can limit your options too early.
Steve Farnworth

Don't be afraid to take the long road. Deep learning has merit. Stick up for yourself. Know that there are numerous opportunities in the world beyond your current bubble.
Matt Sencenbaugh

Make sure you admire the right role models. Sadly, our society celebrates foul values (money, fame, power) and completely disregards the invisible, everyday heroes that work hard to make our lifestyle possible. Take pride in being an everyday hero.
Mel Gilmore

Spend more time considering the people you work with, and less the job or the pay.
Amrita Gurney

Authority is hard-earned but mostly an illusion. Dare to challenge everybody anytime for a better solution, because the things you bring to the table are uniquely yours.
Karl Badde

Don't be afraid to ask for help or show your willingness to learn. Be open and curious!
Mirjam

Chase peers and mentors with original perspectives. It's easy to confuse 'cool' companies and people with those that'll genuinely push your abilities.
Brendan K.

Just be curious. Approach everything you encounter with an attitude of 'Huh, isn't that interesting?'
Brendan Raftery

Knock on doors.
Anastasia S.

When it comes to love, life, and work, invest in the long term.
Kush D.

Don't chase the money. You spend too much time at work to suffer it for cash.
Damon Richards

Don't let your career define your self-identity. Regularly ask yourself: if I lose my ability to work tomorrow, am I still proud of the life I lead? ●
Bhavika Shri

Workspace
TwentyThree

Location
Copenhagen, Denmark

Design & Photography
Årstiderne Arkitekter

Location
New York, NY, USA

Design
Desai Chia Architecture

Photography
Mark Craemer

Quartz

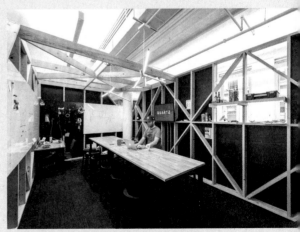

Droids on Roids

Location
Wrocław, Poland

Design
mode:lina

Photography
Patryk Lewiński

Stereo D

Location
Toronto, ON, CA

Design
Quadrangle

Photography
Bob Gundu,
Richard Johnson

emetriq

Location
Hamburg, Germany

Design
Seel Bobsin Partner (sbp)

Photography
Karsten Knocke

Visit
Impact Hub

We checked in at Impact Hub in Vienna, Austria and asked eight people what they're currently working on.

Joe Mak
I'm a professor specialising in clinical electro-physiology at a medical school in Hong Kong. I own a cat and since I travel a lot I looked for ways to monitor her health. Out of that came Aniwear, a device/app that monitors various bio-signals of animals. I'm in Vienna with a grant to research the European market.

Shawn Ardaiz and Imran Rehman
We are from San Francisco and London, respectively. We are developing an app called bekokoro, which addresses a major problem in today's work culture: the lack of feedback and transparency in companies. *Kokoro* is the Japanese concept of the integration of the heart, mind, and soul. Our app creates tight feedback loops within teams, and a safe space for employees to speak up.

Klaudia Bachinger
When my grandmother retired from farm work, she became depressed and almost lost her identity. It motivated me to work on a new online platform called WisR. It'll be a marketplace for the elderly to find project-based or part-time work, and for companies to get access to a treasure trove of experience. Impact Hub has been an incubator for me. It feels like home.

Wendelin Amtmann
I co-founded a bookkeeping app called Chill Bill.
I've been self-employed since the age of 18. It
started with an event company – which I also
still run. Bookkeeping was always a nuisance,
so I created my own solution. Since our first
prototype in 2014, things have grown quickly:
we now have seven employees and an office.
I like coming back here, where it all started.

Anna Reschreiter
I run annatsu, an online business focused on
nutrition coaching and traditional Chinese
medicine. I'm currently mapping out projects
for next year. With a seven-month-old, getting
away from home once a week is essential
to me. I get a lot of work done in the motivating atmosphere here, and my husband and
our son both love their weekly boys' day.

Dimitrios Prodromou
I moved to Vienna in 2007 to study
Mechatronics/Robotics. After seeing the
humanoid robot Pepper at a trade fair, I
decided to co-found Humanizing Technologies
which develops software for Pepper. We're
trying to strike a balance between commercial uses and research. Right now we're
collaborating with a university in Graz to see
how we can help people with dementia.

Ratul Prakash Saha
I'm from Bangladesh and I came here for
a Master's in Renewable Energy Systems.
I grew up in Dhaka, right next to the river
Buriganga, one of the world's ten most polluted
waterways. There's a massive shortage of
clean drinking water, and limited access to
electricity. I'm currently working on a self-sus-
taining water cleaning plant. I hope I can
go back one day and change things. ●

The design researcher
calls on agencies to
rediscover their voice
and take a stand.

Erika
Hall

INTERVIEW
Kai Brach

PHOTOGRAPHY
Derek Yarra

Erika Hall believes that design is in a crisis. Independent voices with a genuine, long-term interest in solving problems are being driven away from the industry by the pervasive influence of venture capital. The co-founder of San Francisco-based digital agency Mule Design believes we need to change the way we talk about and practice design if we're to overcome the challenges now and ahead. For Erika, it all starts with research: only by asking critical, objective questions and having principled but loosely-held opinions can design – and technology – help deliver the promise of a brighter future.

After finishing your degree in philosophy and doing a couple of odd jobs here and there, you worked your way through a few different agencies. What experiences determined the type of agency you wanted to create with Mule?

I think it's all about the people I met during that time. They were crucial to shaping my understanding of the industry, but more so of the type of environment I wanted to work in.

I met a lot of energetic and inspiring people fairly early in my career, like Jared Braiterman, who taught me a lot about working with others and how research should be a natural part of every project. My book *Just Enough Research* is a result of having had those interactions. People like him helped me think creatively about solving problems and how to do it thoughtfully and collaboratively.

On the other hand, what also really influenced me was meeting people who were quite anti-authoritarian. People who didn't hesitate to speak up when someone would throw up roadblocks or say things like, "That's not your job!" It was often some cool, young guy who was hired to tell others that they are full of shit. He was there to expose blind spots. And at one point I realised that I could be that person, because I really like challenging authority. I thought maybe someone would hire me to point out when a decision is made based on fear or because it's just a comfortable way of doing things. Being that blind spot detector is a big part of what we're doing today here at Mule.

So I think meeting these two different types of people – one inspiring and collaborative, the other resistant and more sceptical – was most important.

It's been *sixteen years* since you started Mule. How is working in the client services industry today different from when you first started out?

Every year or so I come across an essay that proclaims that client services are dead or that the golden age of user experience is over. Of course, that's bullshit. What's true is that stuff keeps changing because technology is changing and we are changing.

At the moment there is a huge churn in agencies because a lot of clients now understand the digital design field much better and tend to hire in-house designers and other tech roles. Then there is also the fact that a lot of interaction patterns have been solved or have been commodified. For an ecommerce experience, clients will now just turn to existing apps and tools rather than hiring an agency to try to re-invent the wheel.

The side effect is that it made hiring good people more difficult for agencies. Being a designer in an agency is often more challenging, because the lion's share of your job is to explain why you're solving a problem in a particular way. You can't just sit in front of your thirty-inch monitor with your headphones on thinking, 'Dealing with people is not my job.' That's why a lot of designers or developers think the client is the enemy. The client 'just doesn't understand', and so working in-house at a company seems like an appealing alternative.

I think the agency role today is a much more holistic one. It's not so much about solving a particular technology problem as it is about solving a communication or people problem. Our job is to really listen, to ask difficult questions, to figure out what the client wants to achieve, and then to use a wide range of problem-solving skills to get there.

A lot of people have heard of Mule because they saw a talk or read an essay by you or your co-founder Mike Monteiro. Both of you are known for being strongly opinionated about ethical conduct in our industry. How do you respond to those who say 'leave the politics out of it'?

Design is inherently political, because design is about making choices. Anytime you're making choices, you're in an ethical position, and even more so when you're making choices on behalf of thousands or potentially millions of people. Today, the field of design is such that we're not creating standalone artefacts – we're designing complex systems, and these systems often have unintended consequences. Everything is potentially interconnected with other things.

I have an Amazon Echo at home that essentially listens to everything being said in the room. It's worth keeping in mind that this device was created by a company whose chief executive also owns a very influential newspaper, *The Washington Post*. So you have a listening device *and* a media company run by a mogul who increasingly looks like some sort of James Bond villain. My point is: nothing exists in isolation anymore.

As a designer, you're making choices that further down the track constrain other people's choices. If you can't see how that's a powerful ethical position to be in, you shouldn't be in that position in the first place. That's why I think good designers have to have a strong point of view based on principle. At the same time, they need to be ready to be wrong. 'Strong opinions, loosely held' is one of my favourite phrases. It perfectly describes the characteristics of a good designer. You have to be willing to go out there and argue your point, but then be willing to back down when you realise you're wrong. That's how you solve problems.

Do you think more agencies should follow Mule's example and take a clearer stand?

It's not about following us, it's about giving yourself the leeway to challenge and to question things. Since we just talked about how the agency landscape has changed, I think it's worth pointing out that the voice of design is no longer coming from agencies. The loudest, most prominent design voice is coming out of the Silicon Valley startup world, and that poses a real problem: you can't be a venture-capital-funded startup and at the same time critique growth capitalism or question its sustainability. If you're a designer working for a well-funded tech firm, your ability to

take a stand on ethical conduct with regard to privacy, for example, may be very limited.

Don't get me wrong, I think venture capital is often necessary to bring large-scale ideas to fruition, but all too often, startups take a shallow view of design as a means to increase their valuation. Because, let's be honest, early-stage investors don't have an incentive to care deeply about the problem at hand. They are not funding sustainable businesses; they are funding high-risk investment vehicles. Once they've achieved their return on investment, through acquisition or IPO, they are out. This model only rewards solving problems that scale in a particular way. As a designer, it's very hard to align your long-term vision of providing something meaningful and useful to the world with that drive for rapid growth and the ultimate exit.

Traditionally, a lot of graphic design agencies offered an alternative voice to that, especially here in the Bay Area. But that industry is shrinking and the voices are being drowned out. And, of course, graphic design is a tricky place to critique interactive design from. I think we need more agencies to find their voice again, to find themselves again. That would help solve the existential crisis many agencies are currently going through.

By being very open about your political views, you might not reach certain types of clients willing to challenge those views. Do you think that limits the impact you can have?

It's true, I think our clients self-select because our politics are on the surface, though we do get the occasional request from people on the other side of the values spectrum.

I remember, about ten years ago, some hard-core Republican bloggers approached us. We had a few email exchanges in which we basically tried to make them go away – I mean we're hard-left progressives verging on socialists. But they kept insisting and eventually said, "You can just cash the cheque and not tell anyone, we won't mind." And we were like, "*That's* the difference between us!" This *is* the work. We don't accept money to work on projects that we're ashamed to share publicly.

A few years ago, we received an RFP (request for proposal) from the well-known Hollywood gossip site TMZ. It would have been a big project for us, and technically an interesting one too since they do a lot of breaking 'news'. But when we discussed it internally – which is one of our tenets, to get everyone involved in the business development process – we just didn't know how we would explain it to our other clients. We work with a lot of respected media and journalism organisations and having TMZ on that list would have felt like a big middle finger to them.

We often justify working for those companies believing we can effect change from the inside. Can that be a valid argument for taking on morally questionable jobs?

It all comes down to how the money is made. As a designer, you're hired to help them meet a business goal. If the company makes money by creating harm, you're not going to talk them out of it – unless you re-engineer their entire business model. At Mule, instead of *user-centred* design, we talk a lot more about *value-centred* design. With the former, the focus lies on empathy: how to give users a great experience. Being empathetic is great, but an interaction is more multifaceted than that. A casino offers a perfect user-centred design experience, but it's still a casino. It's still doing a lot of harm. With a value-centred design approach, you're not just looking at the user, but also what the business gets out of it, and whether it's a fair exchange of value.

As a designer, you can analyse that exchange: if the business is extracting something from its users, what is the business offering in exchange? We have no problem with the business making money, but it has to offer something of *positive* value to their customers, and, ideally, create something of positive value for the world. It's the designer's job to make that exchange more beneficial for everyone. But if the equation is such that the business extracts money by doing something unethical with no positive value to its users, then there's no point in taking on the job.

It's easy for established agencies or freelancers to be picky about the clients they choose to work with. For people just starting out, do you think it's acceptable to sacrifice some principles in order to get a foot in the door?

No, I think the opposite is true. Of course, not every client we've worked with in the past has been a world-changing social enterprise – sometimes you take on jobs that are on fairly 'neutral' moral ground that you accept because they pay well. However, being selective very early on is important because those first jobs send a signal to the clients you want to work with. If your first few clients have dubious business models, you quickly become the go-to person for that kind of work. Having said that, I totally understand how hard it is to get started. It's important to remember, though, that the whole reason for running your own business is to have that freedom to choose who you'd like to work with. We started Mule because the agencies we previously worked with didn't always make decisions about their clients the way we would. We

realised that choosing the right clients makes you who you are as an agency. And along the way, we've made our own mistakes as well.

What's interesting about working with clients that feel strongly about 'doing the right thing' is that decision-making may be driven by politics, ego, or ideology. When you deal with for-profit businesses it's easy to build your arguments around maximising profit: 'Doing this will make you more money!' But with non-profits or social enterprises there is a lot more nuance involved. There is a different dynamic at play that isn't as straightforward as working with someone just selling something.

In one of your talks you stated that "designers must also be philosophers". What exactly do you mean by that?

This goes back to what I mentioned earlier about how as a designer you are setting up choices for other people. Studying philosophy is all about thinking through counterfactual scenarios, which is pretty much exactly what you're doing as a designer. You conjure alternative scenarios and ask, 'What would happen

if we created a system that worked like *that*?'

I think designers need to start at the thought experiment stage rather than rushing to make prototypes. It leads to better decisions. Another big part of philosophy is asking questions, constructing an argument, and then testing that argument for its validity.

With that approach you can identify issues much earlier and more cheaply than actually creating the thing and then feeling like you have to defend your decision because of the sunk cost involved.

So, in other words, we're not going deep enough. Perhaps we need to change the way we talk about design?

Absolutely. I feel a lot of designers believe that by improving their technique, they can get off the hook for not being good at other things, like design critique for instance. A big part of what's causing this lack of depth is that today design as a discipline is a team effort.

Our design heroes of the past, like Paul Rand or the Eameses, had full control over their work and, consequently, took responsibility for the decisions that went into it. Today, we rarely do design as individuals anymore. We're building these complex systems with huge teams and any one person contributes only a part. That's what makes going deep and taking a stand so difficult.

Also, today – at least in the Western world – there are far fewer things that really *need* design than we think. Look at the impact of smartphones, for example. One device has made a whole list of other products redundant. Our smartphones have replaced our watch, our camera, our alarm clock, our radio, et cetera. Apple has already made a lot of design decisions for us which means our latitude as designers in the traditional sense is highly constrained. Sure, you can design your own product on that platform, but Apple's interface conventions dictate what you can or can't do.

If your phone does all those things so well already, what problem is there to solve? The response to that are the many silly ideas our industry comes up with – from laundry delivery apps to smart salt shakers. We've fixed all the easy things; now the bar for issues that really need solving is incredibly high. So we make up 'problems'.

In one of your recent essays you claim that anxiety in the design process has a flow-on effect that increases the potential for anxiety in the world. Can you give us some examples for how this plays out in practice?

From working with lots of different organi-sations over the years we've found that many decisions are made not based on research, data, or just common sense, but on fear and anxiety. When a business reacts to a compet-itor by adding certain features not because of a specific value to their customers but instead because of the fear they will be left behind, this leads to bad decisions further down the road. It causes designers to create artefacts that aren't inherently useful or valuable to their customers. So you end up with a product that is bloated and confusing and, eventually, creates anxiety for the user. Products built on these anxie-ty-driven design choices are often flawed and therefore short-lived. But it doesn't stop there.

When companies are quick to copy their competitors out of fear and desperation, it can lead to so-called 'me-too-ism'. What you get is a huge amount of undifferentiated products to choose from. Have you ever been to the toothpaste aisle at a large supermarket? Here in the US, you have about eighty toothpastes to choose from with little to no difference between them. It makes me anxious just thinking about it.

Another great example: communication. So many businesses are afraid of being concise in the way they communicate with their customers. Rather than expressing them-selves clearly, they often prefer dumping huge amounts of information on their customers. It's amazing how often we can summarise a message in a few words, but the client's response would be, 'We need more text here.'

Where does that need to be verbose come from? It's a fear of not looking smart, of appearing too simple. Too often compa-nies try to prove their value by seeming clever and 'professional'. They don't realise that this is one of the biggest barriers to actually achieving their goals, and it leaves the user overwhelmed and frustrated.

Understanding the importance of research in the design process can help avoid going down that rabbit hole. For those who haven't read your book, what is design research and what is it not?

I think the word 'research' can cause a bit of confusion. It's often seen as something that must result in earth-shattering, new knowledge about the world in order to justify the work. That's a different standard of research. That's more the purview of academic research, which often follows rigorous protocols and leads to extensive reports at the end. Unfortunately, that standard gets misapplied to design.

The point of research in design is just to get the information you need to be able to fully understand and then solve the problem at hand. We've come up with a lot of ways to talk about design and most of them avoid this simple fact: you can't practice design genuinely without having done your research.

With my book I wanted to highlight that design research might not take more than a couple of days at a time, and it probably doesn't require a lengthy report. There are certainly no focus groups in depressing research rooms. It's a tool that helps you optimise for the right things and figure out what you know and what you don't know. As such, the most important outcome may just be a list of fundamental questions you would have missed asking if you hadn't done the research.

The title *Just Enough Research* was intentionally chosen to show that the minimum amount of research can be sufficient, because you're not doing this for the sake of research itself – you're doing it for the sake of design. To be honest, the book exists because I was just getting tired of explaining to people why it is such a crucial part of design practice.

Current location
San Francisco, CA USA

Hometown
Los Angeles, CA, USA

Top bookmarks
medium.com, twitter.com, wikipedia.com, google.com, theguardian.com

Top apps
Twitter, Instagram, Zoom, Youtube, WhatsApp

Recommended reading
Behave by Robert Sapolsky, *The Woman Who Borrowed Memories* by Tove Jansson, *Autonomous* by Annalee Newitz

Inspired by
Someone new every day. Anyone who manages to be kind to other people, no matter what life serves. That is harder than platitudes would have it.

Favourite accessory
If I said anything other than my chug Rupert, everyone would know I was lying.

Tea or coffee
Coffee. Drip. Strong, splash of milk. Have a Technivorm-Moccamaster at home and at the studio. Best coffeemaker.

On the web
muledesign.com

How do we go about asking questions which aren't inherently biased?

We all naturally want to be proven right. If your goal is to verify your theory, then you'll automatically pick out the parts of the research that will help you achieve that. In that case, why bother doing it at all? But if you can swap that around in your head and go into your research by asking, 'How can I *disprove* my theory?', then you may end up with surprising results.

This is why philosophy and design go so well together. Philosophers start out by putting forth an argument and then they try hard to take that argument apart, knowing that it'll make the end result stronger. And not just that – they invite others to join them in that process of deconstructing their argument. Collaboration is a hugely important element, and it's something we should always look for in design research.

You always want to start with a lot of clarity about your goal. What's your goal for doing the design in the first place? With your goal in mind, you'll be able to identify any potential risks and assumptions you're making along the way. From there you'll get your research questions, and, again, you want to phrase them in a way that will test those assumptions, not confirm them. So, for instance, make sure you ask open-ended, not leading questions.

Typical marketing surveys provide great examples of bad research questions. I take every survey I come across and, oh boy, almost all of them are terrible because they're engineered to provide satisfying answers. We have so many apps and tools at our disposal, and most of them encourage us to create surveys focused on quantity of data, not quality. None of them allows participants to ask follow-up questions, so if your research questions are terrible, there is no way you'll ever find out. You gathered data for the sake of counting data.

What does a quality-over-quantity approach look like and how do we make sure we're reaching the right people?

To get better quality results there is a very simple solution: talk to people. And to make sure you are talking to the right ones, you follow the exact same principles I just described: you establish what your assumptions are and figure out the biggest risks of being wrong.

We once had a client that targeted all their marketing towards a specific demographic. When we asked them what this decision was based on, there was suddenly a lot of nervous shuffling because they realised they'd made it up. It turned out that they picked that demographic because it matched the demographic of their own team. They targeted specific people because those were the only ones they could relate to. So we went out there and tested those assumptions and – big surprise – they were totally wrong. Sometimes disproving a hypothesis is as easy as picking at a simple statement.

More practically speaking, to get better research results you can use tools like Ethnio to screen a group of people first, and then follow up on the phone. You find participants who do certain things, or claim to do certain things, and then discuss their actions individually to better understand them. Then you continue to iterate based on your results.

That's perhaps one of the most important things I wanted to make clear with my book: research is not just a single task you do once in the design process. It's a habit. Yes, we do initial research at the start of the project, but it doesn't stop there. We don't have a 'special research mode'; it's just an integral part of our practice that continues throughout any project. At any point we might say, 'OK, this looks solid. Now let's talk to at least ten people to see how it holds up.'

It seems that in order to achieve minimal bias in design we all need a lesson in humility. We need to learn to shut our egos out of the process.

Humility is crucial. There is a strange, unwarranted pressure for designers to be confident decision makers and to magically know exactly which solutions are the right ones. The reality is, though, that unless you're designing something to solve a problem that's unique to you, you need to take your opinions out of it.

For most designers it's really easy to go down the path of self-indulgence because they like control over things. They believe design is the process of exerting control, but it's really not. Design is the process of understanding how to seek control in order to create something that's useful to a lot of people. To be a successful designer you have to understand how people who are totally not like you function.

To instil more humility we need to change the way we evaluate design. We are still hung up on doing work that looks good in a portfolio. When we 'design for delight', what we're really doing is showing off our technique. Instead of designing yet another delightful mobile app that vies for our attention, we should look for ways to move more seamlessly through the world so that we can pay attention to the things that matter.

If you're a good designer today, chances are that no one will remember your work. That's because you may have only contributed a small part to an enormous, complex, interactive system. You're part of a large team that critically and strategically thinks about the goal of your business or organisation. It's not sexy and you won't have anything flashy to show for it at the end.

Still talking about minimising bias, how important is being mindful of the language we use?

Injecting your own bias into the phrasing of your questions is a big issue, of course. I've always been critical of using jargon of any type, because it separates us into in-groups and out-groups, and by doing that we naturally exclude certain people.

Beyond research or design, it's just really important to understand how our words impact other people. When I recently read some of Microsoft's user interface guidelines, a section

was using 'your mother' as an example for a less tech-savvy person. It's not just a dumb cliché, but it also makes you ask whether they have ever wondered how many of their female employees are mothers themselves? Or here's a less tech-related example: the beauty product line Dove sells a skincare product that says 'good for normal to dark skin' on its label. The assumption, of course, is that light skin is normal and dark skin is not.

So if you're part of the assumed in-group, you won't really notice when things slip in that are extremely exclusionary. And that can have pretty devastating consequences – not just for the business, but for other people. Always ask yourself: what is assumed to be the default and what is assumed to be the outlier? If you're part of the default, your thinking is probably biased.

Do you think that some biases, in particular those that lead to racial or gender inequality, are more pronounced in our industry than in others?

I don't think they are. Look at what just happened in the movie industry – with Harvey Weinstein being only the tip of the iceberg.

However, the fact that these issues even exist in the tech world is particularly distressing because we're supposed to be the ones creating a better future.

There has always been this belief that big tech companies can bring about a brighter, more just future for all. But it turns out that, at best, they are ridden with the same problems, and, at worst, they can in fact exacerbate social issues. When companies receive billions in funding to 'create the future', but then only hire representatives of a narrow segment of society, those who are left out feel frustrated and angry in the face of a broken promise. Of course, this situation gets increasingly terrifying as more and more systems are automated. If we use this flawed base-knowledge as a building block for artificial intelligence, it's going to be incredibly difficult to root out later on.

It all connects back to what we discussed before: if you don't start from this place of critique and realise how much influence you have as a designer of these systems, then it's really easy to coast on assumptions. When you've always been part of the in-group, you may be totally ignorant of the fact that your work is amplifying some very bad things indeed. •

If you're a good designer today, chances are that no one will remember your work. That's because you may have only contributed a small part to an enormous, complex, interactive system. You're part of a large team that critically and strategically thinks about the goal of your business or organisation. It's not sexy and you won't have anything flashy to show for it at the end.

Erika Hall

Cameron is a founding partner of design and engineering studio Fictive Kin, based in Brooklyn, NY. You may know him as the co-organiser of a web conference called Brooklyn Beta and the creator of a simple to-do app called TeuxDeux.

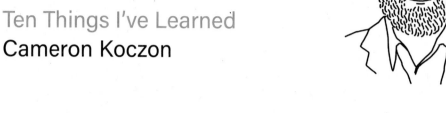

Ten Things I've Learned
Cameron Koczon

1 The economics of a service company are crazy. It took me forever to realise that bigger agencies don't necessarily make more money than smaller ones on a per-partner basis. So why try to be huge? Stay small and happy. You can still do great things and make good money.

2 It takes an editor to get your best writing done. Nobel Prize winner Toni Morrison said, "Good editors are really the third eye. Cool. Dispassionate. They don't love you or your work." Matches my experience perfectly.

3 Running a conference is hard, as I learned from co-organising Brooklyn Beta for five years. I am going to die much younger because of it. With most creative work, you share it when it feels solid enough. An event, however, unfolds in real time before your eyes. You discover whether it's any good at the exact same time the audience does.

4 When it comes to emails, slow means no. If you're waiting on an overdue reply, assume it's a 'no' and plan/act accordingly. If it turns out to be a 'yes', it'll be a happy little surprise.

5 Film director John Cassavetes told me two important things: true humour can't come out of anything but hard work, and great collaborative work comes about when people are able to stay individuals and keep thinking.

6 There's a difference between output and activity. Output is what matters, but the world focuses on activity.

7 Don't give your software away for free. When we started charging for TeuxDeux, we lost a whole bunch of *users* but gained an amazing group of *customers*. We were also suddenly able to make improvements and fix broken things. The ones who stayed (more than enough) are having a great time.

8 I've been obsessed with what I call 'the principle of enough' – run your business so that you make enough instead of the most. Enough is plenty, I usually say. Then last week I saw Mary Poppins say, "Enough is a feast", and I knew I had my life mantra.

9 Money has its own velocity. The speed at which it comes in is relative to the speed at which it goes out. If you earn twenty dollars from an hour of work, you will spend that money more slowly than if you find a twenty-dollar bill on the street. This relationship plays out in all kinds of interesting ways in business.

10 "Slow is smooth and smooth is fast." It's something my military friends and family say. Slowing down goes against our instinctive approach to progress, but managing to do so has been instrumental in how we work at Fictive Kin.

Unn is a Swedish user experience designer
at design firm Doberman and co-organiser
of the meet-up Designers in Stockholm. She
loves horses and human-friendly tech.

Unn Swanström

1 A simple trick for the socially anxious:
instead of worrying about whether a
person you just met likes you or not,
focus on *them* instead. Mutual liking
stems from finding shared interests. Be
curious, ask questions, and truly listen.

2 Companies are just collections of people.
Don't get bamboozled by fancy branding or
plush offices. Focus on finding a group of
people that will help you do your best work.

3 Swedish people love a good *fika*, which
is short for sitting down with someone
for coffee and pastry. Science says
that we are better problem solvers if
we take regular breaks. *Fika* it up!

4 Creativity is a fragile process. The
most important factor in achieving
great results as a team is psycholog-
ical safety. Every team member must
feel that she or he can share their most
bizarre ideas without being ridiculed.

5 Knowing how to communicate effectively
is a lifelong learning process – not just
at work. I recently discovered the power
of 'relationship retros' with my significant
other at home, and it made us a better
couple. (In case you don't know, 'retro-
spectives' or 'retros' are team meetings to
evaluate what has worked well in the past
and what should be changed in the future).

6 Horses are excellent mindfulness coaches.
There is no time to worry about work when
you're trying to manœuvre hundreds of
kilograms of cantering muscle power.

7 Great solutions often stem from extreme
and weird ideas. In our studio, we prototype and test several ideas that are way
out there before dialing it down in the final
concept. We call them 'provocatypes' – a
great way to stretch your imagination and
not settle for the first, most obvious choice.

8 Knowing when to send the appro-
priate animal gif is an important
twenty-first-century life skill.

9 Don't be too protective of your creations.
Always ask for feedback early in your
creative process. By letting other people
in, you avoid getting overly attached
to one particular solution, which may
not be the most elegant or efficient.

10 Remember that you are the designer
of your life. Don't make assumptions
about love, work, and lifestyle based
on what other people enjoy or what is
expected of you. Iterate! Make changes
until you find what works for *you*. ●

Patrons

A Adam Lee
adaml.ee

Alex Cornell
alexcornell.com

Alfred Nerstu
alfrednerstu.com

Antoine Llorca
llor.ca

Artiom Dashinsky
twitter.com/hvost

August
august.com.au

B Bakken & Bæck
bakkenbaeck.com

beyond tellerrand
beyondtellerrand.com

Björn Jensen
improuv.com

Booom.
booom.studio

Bright
bright.io

Built With Code
builtwithcode.com

C Carrie Ford Hilliker
fordvisuals.com

Chapter
chaptersf.com

Character
ofcharacter.com

chendo
chen.do

Chris Meisner
chrismeisner.com

Christian Koch
christiankoch.nyc

Claimable
claimable.com

Contrast
contrast.co

Creative Soapbox
creativesoapbox.com

D Daily JOMO
dailyjomo.com

Damien Newman
centralstory.com

Damien Senger
raccoon.studio

Dapper Notes
dappernotes.com

Dave & Brit Morin
morin.com

Diego Fernandez
diego.gs

Do Equals Glory

Dominik Väyrynen
dominikvayrynen.com

Drew Hamlin
drewhamlin.com

E Early Days
earlydays.com

Element AI
elementai.com

Emily Dela Cruz
emilydelacruz.com

Engine Digital
enginedigital.com

Erzgebirge-Palace
erzgebirgepalace.com

F Febril Cuevas
febril.co

Flume for Instagram
flumeapp.com

Francisco Deus
franciscodeus.pt

Franco Papeschi

Friends
bff.co

Full Stack Films
fullstackfilms.com.au

Fúnksjón vefráðgjöf
funksjon.net

G Good People
goodpeople.productions

Grayscale Ltd
grayscale.com.hk

Grégory de Jonckheere
nckh.com

Guillaume Berry
somanyknobs.net

H hedgehog lab
hedgehoglab.com

Holoscribe
holoscribe.com

Honestly
honestly.co

Honor
joinhonor.com

Hudl
hudl.com

Humaan
humaan.com

Humana Design
humana.design

I Indianapolis Coffee Guide
indianapoliscoffeeguide.com

J Jan Kovařík
jankovarik.net

K King Louis
kinglouiscreative.com

Kreativgebiet
kreativgebiet.com

L Lacompany
lacompany.com

Liliana Castro
fesagency.pt

liquidmoon
liquidmoon.de

Lookahead Search
lookahead.com.au

Looksie Optometry
looksieoptometry.com

Lucid
lucid.nz

M Maple Inside
mapleinside.com

Metabahn
metabahn.com

Michael Novak
michael.novak.org

Mike Stephen
essentiallymike.com

MileIQ
mileiq.com

O Obscure Design Co
obscuredesign.co

Owen van Dijk
owenvandijk.co

P Pasilobus, Inc
pasilobus.com

Paul Stefan Ort
pso.io

Perioperative Consulting
perioperative.com.au

Pixelgrade
pixelgrade.com

Playbook
askplaybook.com

Ploink
plo.ink

pooliestudios
pooliestudios.com

pr+co Corporate Publishing
prco.de

Process Masterclass
process-masterclass.com

R Reaktor
reaktor.com

revise
revise.cc

S Samuel Ericson Design
samuelericson.com

Sean Sharp
seansharp.org

Seçkin Kılıç
seck.in

Seth Cheeks
sethcheeks.com

SimpleBits
simplebits.com

T Terence Bergagna
casafortegroup.com

thoughtbot
thoughtbot.com

Threadless
threadless.com

Till Leinen
till.is

Patrons

Travis CI
travis-ci.com

U Underbelly
underbelly.is

V Via Studios
viastudios.co.uk

W Wake
wake.com

We Help Chiros
wehelpchiros.com

Webactually
webactually.com

webfactory GmbH
webfactory.de

Whitespace
whitespace.se

Wildbit, LLC
wildbit.com

Y Yuvl Gupta

Z Zach Grosser
zachgrosser.com

zeit:raum digital
zeitraum.com

A big 'thank you' goes out to every patron subscriber for their generous contribution! Support Offscreen and add your name to this list: offscreenmag.com/patrons

Special thanks also to Agnes Lee, Alice Default, Derek Yarra, Ivana McConnell, Kamila Schneltser Pinilla, Kieran O'Hare, Martin Holtkamp, Michelle Fan, Shayan Asgharnia, Sina Diehl, the many readers who continue to send in feedback and supportive words, and everyone else who helped make this issue come together.

And of course, once again, our sincere gratitude goes out to our sponsors, without whom Offscreen would not exist: Adobe Typekit, Balsamiq, Harvest, Hover, MailChimp, SiteGround, Swarm, and Ueno.

Contributor Index

Join the Offscreen club.

If you enjoyed this issue please consider supporting our efforts to create a more thoughtful and human-centred tech community by becoming a subscriber. offscreenmag.com/subscribe

To stay connected in between issues, sign up to *Offscreen Dispatch*, our free weekly newsletter featuring exciting new projects, apps, and accessories. offscreenmag.com/dispatch